RANGERS
LEAD THE WAY

Pointe-du-Hoc D-Day 1944

STEVEN J. ZALOGA

First published in 2009 by Osprey Publishing
Midland House, West Way, Botley, Oxford OX2 0PH, UK
443 Park Avenue South, New York, NY 10016, USA
E-mail: info@ospreypublishing.com

ISBN 978 1 84603 394 0
E-book ISBN: 978 1 84908 102 3

Page layout by: Bounford.com, Cambridge, UK
Index by Alan Thatcher
Typeset in Sabon
Maps by The Map Studio
3D BEVs by The Black Spot
Originated by PPS Grasmere Ltd, Leeds, UK
Printed in China through Worldprint

09 10 11 12 13   10 9 8 7 6 5 4 3 2 1

A CIP catalog record for this book is available from the British Library

AUTHOR'S NOTE

The author would like to thank Dr Simon Trew of the Royal Military Academy Sandhurst for his generous supply of documents from his own research on Pointe-du-Hoc. Thanks also go to David Fletcher of the Tank Museum, Bovington, J. Desautels, Roger Cirillo, and Dr Philip Blood for their help on this project.

THE WOODLAND TRUST

Osprey Publishing are supporting the Woodland Trust, the UK's leading woodland conservation charity, by funding the dedication of trees.

EDITOR'S NOTE

For ease of comparison between types, Imperial/American measurements are used almost exclusively throughout this book. The following data will help in converting the Imperial/American measurements to metric:

1 mile = 1.6km

1lb = 0.45kg

1yd = 0.9m

1ft = 0.3m

1in = 2.54cm/25.4mm

1gal = 4.5 liters

1 ton (US) = 0.9 tonnes

CONTENTS

INTRODUCTION

The German gun battery on the rocky promontory of Pointe-du-Hoc was feared as the most dangerous threat to the D-Day landings in Normandy, able to menace the amphibious landings at Omaha and Utah Beaches. The extensive fortification of the battery in 1943–44 prevented airborne assault from landward. Instead, the 2nd Rangers were assigned to make an amphibious landing, surmount the cliffs under enemy fire, and then assault and destroy the gun positions.

Pointe-du-Hoc is a classic example of a seemingly impossible mission being accomplished by a stalwart band of elite troops in the face of overwhelming odds. The success of the Ranger raid on the position on D-Day has become an American military legend, enshrined as a model of American military valor on a par with Bunker Hill and Gettysburg. Yet controversy has bubbled under the surface of the legend. The Rangers did not find the guns in their fortifications on Pointe-du-Hoc, but discovered them unattended more than a mile away. Moreover, was the raid really necessary? This book seeks to re-examine the mission by extending the focus beyond the undoubted heroics of the Rangers to examine unexplored aspects, including the seldom studied German perspective and the role of the Allied air forces and navies in subduing Pointe-du-Hoc.

In August 1942, Allied aerial reconnaissance first discovered that the Wehrmacht had positioned three medium guns on the heights of Pointe-du-Hoc, a rocky outcropping on the lower Normandy coast near the small port of Grandcamp-les-Bains on the eastern side of the Vire River estuary. It was also known as the St-Pierre-du-Mont battery on account of the nearest village, or by one of its local spellings, Pointe-du-Hoe; Grandcamp today is called Grandcamp-Maisy.

In May 1943, the French resistance group *Confrérie Notre-Dame* (Notre-Dame Brotherhood) sent a map to London that had been stolen from German offices in Caen; the plan detailed the intended construction of *Atlantikwall* (Atlantic Wall) fortifications in the lower Normandy area. This map ended up in the hands of Chief of Staff Supreme Allied Command (COSSAC), who had been assigned the task of planning Operation *Neptune*, the forthcoming amphibious invasion of France. The coast of lower Normandy from Caen west to the Contentin peninsula seemed especially suitable for Operation *Neptune* because of the weak coastal artillery defenses, and the stolen map provided clear evidence. Upper Normandy and the Pas-de-Calais were nearer to Britain, so the *Atlantikwall* fortifications were much thicker in this area, as was the concentration of German combat units. Was the Caen map genuine? For the next several months, Allied photo reconnaissance charted the course of German construction along the lower Normandy coast and found that the map did indeed correspond to German fortification activities. A special intelligence cell in London collated the data and issued periodic "Martian" reports detailing the fortification efforts for COSSAC as the *Neptune* plan took shape.

Concern over the coastal batteries was heightened due to recent changes in technology, especially the advent of radar. In the past, amphibious operations could use the cover of night to cloak the massing of transport ships off the coast, especially during their most vulnerable phase when the transports were stationary as they unloaded the infantry into landing craft in the "Transport Area." Coastal artillery, now linked to maritime surface-search radars, stripped away the cloak of darkness and made it possible for the batteries to engage the transports in the dark. The threat posed by the German coastal batteries and their associated radars to the massing of transports and landing craft was a growing worry to the COSSAC planners, as Kriegsmarine (navy) radar sites began springing up along the French coast.

Once lower Normandy was selected as the Allied objective for Operation *Neptune*, the planners began to focus on how to deal with the main coastal artillery threats, especially those batteries that were first completed at Pointe-du-Hoc and Ouistreham. The initial COSSAC plan from August 1943 proposed the use of one US parachute battalion and two Ranger battalions in the Grandcamp area, with the paratroopers assigned to neutralize the Pointe-du-Hoc battery while the Rangers would deal with the two batteries near Maisy. Over the next few months, however, these plans were refined as more intelligence was gathered from France. Information from the French resistance indicated that the Pointe-du-Hoc battery was a dedicated coastal defense unit armed with potent 155mm GPF (*Grand Puissance Filloux*: High-

Six of these 15.5cm Kanone 418(f) at Pointe-du-Hoc were the cause of intense concern to Allied D-Day planners. These were captured French World War I guns, better known as the 155mm GPF. (Alain Chazette)

Powered Filloux) guns, while the neighboring Maisy batteries were divisional artillery batteries armed with less formidable weapons incapable of reaching either the Omaha or Utah Transport Areas. This assessment was further reinforced when the Pointe-du-Hoc battery began extensive fortification in the summer and autumn of 1943. As a result, attention began to center on Pointe-du-Hoc and the associated radar station located on the coast 2½ miles east near Le Guay. Both sites were troublesome for planners, as they were located 90–120ft over the sea on the cliffs so common in this region of Normandy. Assault from the landward side by airborne forces was problematic due to the extent of German defenses against such a threat, including extensive minefields and anti-glider obstacles. As a result, the plans were in a state of flux through late 1943. Although there were some arguments about the best methods of attacking the batteries, there were no doubts that it was vital to eliminate them prior to the main landings.

ORIGINS OF THE RAID

On May 24, 1942, the 2nd battery of HKAA.832 (*Heeres-Küsten-Artillerie-Abteilung*: Army Coastal Artillery Battalion) was transferred from its original position outside Boulogne on the Channel coast to Pointe-du-Hoc in lower Normandy as part of an effort to build up defenses on the Seine Bay. The battery was nominally horse-drawn, though in fact it possessed only four old horses. It was armed with six 15.5cm K 418 guns, the German designation for the French 155mm GPF gun. These were World War I-era heavy artillery pieces captured in 1940 and widely used by German coastal batteries due to their excellent range and firepower. Curiously enough, the US Army had received this weapon from France in 1918 and had manufactured it under license; it was widely used by US Army coastal artillery units in 1941–45 in much the same fashion as the battery at Pointe-du-Hoc. As a result, the US Army was well aware of the capabilities of this weapon in the coastal defense role.

German coastal defense doctrine focused on the defense of ports and accordingly the Pointe-du-Hoc battery was assigned to defend the neighboring port of Grandcamp, as well as the Vire River estuary and its associated harbors, such as Grand Vey. The Germans confiscated the 30-acre site from three local families, with the Guelinel family being evicted from their farmhouse in September 1942. The Guelinel farm was converted to a mess hall, stables, and accommodations for the battery until new barracks could be constructed. The six guns were originally set up in ordinary field positions protected by earthen berms and sandbags, and camouflaged with nets. The battery's nominal table of organization included 6 officers, 20 NCOs, and 120 troops and it was originally commanded by Oberleutnant Frido Ebeling. As the battery was intended to be capable of engaging enemy ships, firing practice was conducted from the site using targets placed on wooden rafts out to sea. The site was initially designated as *Stützpunkt Bayeux* 075 (Bayeux Strongpoint 075).

Fortification of the site began in November 1942 with the arrival of personnel from the Organization Todt (OT), the German paramilitary construction group. The OT team at Pointe-du-Hoc consisted of about 150 German OT workers, reinforced by French and Algerian forced laborers as well as Polish and Russian prisoners-of-war, averaging about 500 men through 1943. Italian troops were added to the construction force in 1944, Italy having switched sides to the Allies. The Pointe-du-Hoc site was covered with the usual Norman "bocage" hedgerows, and these were gradually removed to give the guns clear fields of fire. Construction began on the "officer's bunker," a command post located near the battery entrance at the south end of the site, followed by a H661 medical bunker. As the site was becoming increasingly obvious to Allied intelligence, the next construction was a pair of L409A Flak bunkers on either side to accommodate 3.7cm Flak 36 anti-aircraft cannon. The western Flak bunker was commanded by Unteroffizier Helmut Neder and the eastern site by Erwin Thomalla. The first air attacks on the site by Allied fighter-bombers did not occur until April 1943, and were not especially intense or frequent.

Allied planning for D-Day depended on the elimination of German naval search radars, like this damaged FuMO 2 Calais radar at Kriegsmarine radar station "Imme" in *Stützpunkt Le Guay*, which provided data to the Ponte-du-Hoc battery. (NARA)

This is the H502 personnel bunker for NCOs. It had two rooms with a total capacity of 20 troops and Tobruk circular machine-gun pits for self-defense at either end. (Author)

German coastal defense batteries traditionally used the World War I *Kesselbettungen* (kettle positions), so named on account of the pan-like shape of the reinforced gun pit. These were large, 52ft-wide concrete shelters with two underground niches for ammunition and propellant as well as an attached underground shelter for the gun crew. With the gun pits in place by the summer of 1943, construction began on personnel bunkers, which were modular designs for one or two sections (*Gruppen*) of ten men:

Coastal Defense
Sector H2 (East),
D-Day, June6, 1944

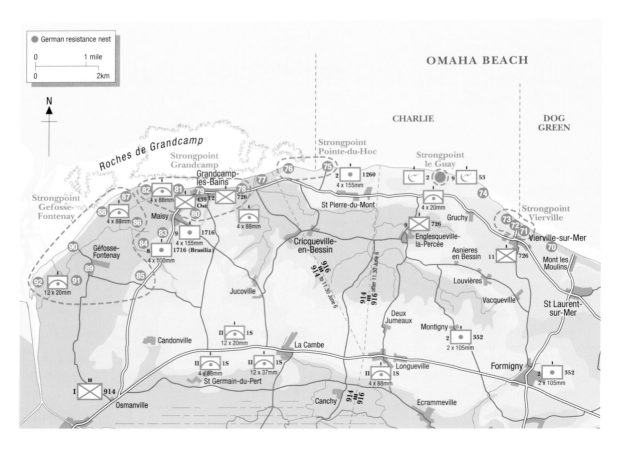

GERMAN DEFENSES AT POINTE-DU-HOC

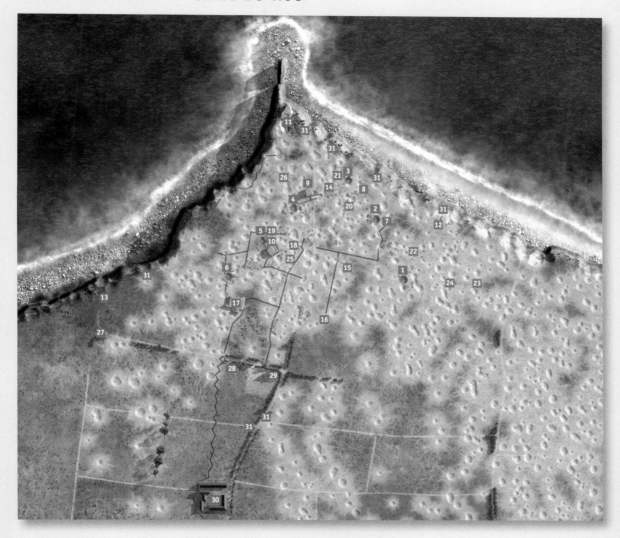

GERMAN FORCES
2./HKAR.1260 (2nd Battalion, Army Coastal Artillery Regiment 1260)

1 Gun pit 1

2 Gun pit 2

3 Gun pit 3

4 Gun pit 4

5 Gun pit 5

6 Gun pit 6

7 H679 Casemate 2 (foundation)

8 H679 Casemate 3 (foundation)

9 H679 Casemate 4

10 H679 Casemate 5

11 H636A Observation bunker

12 East L409A Flak bunker

13 West L409A Flak bunker

14 H134 ammunition bunkers

15 Ammunition storage shed

16 Small ammunition bunker

17 H661 Double-group personnel bunker (20 men)

18 H662 Double-group personnel bunker (20 men)

19 H502 SK Double-group personnel bunker (20 NCO)

20 H621 Group personnel bunker (10 men)

21 Group personnel bunker (10 men)

22 Group personnel bunker (10 men)

23 Tobruk gun pit

24 Troops barracks

25 Open communication trench

26 Covered communication trench

27 Guard tower

28 Abandoned Guelinel farm

29 Post entrance

30 Abandoned farm buildings

31 Machine-gun positions

The cliffs of Pointe-du-Hoc were booby-trapped with "roller-mines" like this one, which consisted of old French artillery projectiles suspended by wires. (MHI)

Gruppenstand or *Doppelgruppenstand*. The designs used at Pointe-du-Hoc were the usual assortment of standardized designs. The architectural designs for the bunkers were often appended with prefixes to identify the branch of service requesting the plan, so the H622 personnel bunker plan indicated an army (Heer) design while the L409 Flak bunker indicated a Luftwaffe design. Most *Atlantikwall* fortifications, including those at Pointe-du-Hoc, were built to the "B" standard, which was 6ft 7in thick of steel-reinforced concrete, intended to be proof against artillery up to 8in and 1,000lb bombs. Many minor bunkers such as the "Tobruk" machine-gun pits were built to the slightly lower B1 standard of 3ft 3in–3ft 11in, as these structures were partially buried.

The 1943 work included the first efforts to build fully enclosed gun casemates for the battery. This was the result of a major shift in fortification policy in the winter of 1942–43 in the aftermath of the August 1942 Dieppe raid, which revealed the vulnerability of the kettle gun pits to air attack. Although the casemates offered better protection for the guns, at the same time they severely limited their traverse. In the case of the Pointe-du Hoc batteries, the selection of the H679 design meant that the guns would have a limited traverse of only 120 degrees (60 degrees to either side). This point is worth noting, as it clearly demonstrates that the guns were intended for seaward defense; the guns could not traverse sufficiently to engage targets on neighboring Omaha Beach or Utah Beach once placed in the casemates. As a compromise, the usual pattern was to place four of the six guns in the casemates while leaving the remaining two in the old kettle positions to provide some all-around coverage.

The winter 1942/43 *Atlantikwall* plan expected that work would be completed by the end of the summer of 1943, so the construction techniques for the casemates were non-standard in order to rush their completion. Instead of the usual method of pouring concrete using wooden shuttering, "shell construction" was used, which consisted of forming the inner and outer walls from small pre-cast concrete blocks and pouring concrete into the void after the Monier steel reinforcing rods were erected inside the void. Work tapered off in the autumn of 1943 due to British attacks on the Ruhr industrial region, which led to large-scale transfers of OT workers back to Germany. In the end, only two of the casemates neared completion, a third was partly finished, and a fourth was excavated but only the floor completed. Supplies of ventilators, electrical fittings, and other accessories never arrived, so none of the casemates was ever actually occupied and the guns remained in their kettle positions.

In August 1943, while the gun casemates were being built, three H134 ammunition bunkers were built. The final major construction was the H636A fire control bunker, completed in October 1943, which was located at the tip of the promontory facing out to sea. It contained an optical range-finder for target acquisition and ranging in a pit on top of the bunker, and communication rooms inside including both radio and field telephone workrooms. This bunker was commanded by Leutnant Wilhelm Ruhl and permanently manned by at least three men. In contrast to the Kriegsmarine fire control bunkers, the army range-finder did not have overhead protection, and the fire control center was rudimentary for dealing with moving naval targets.

While the army battery at Pointe-du-Hoc was being fortified, the Kriegsmarine 2.Funkmessabteilung (Radar Regiment) had established a major surveillance station codenamed "Imme" at *Stützpunkt Le Guay* near the Pointe-et-Raz-de-la-Percée, 2½ miles east. This consisted of a pair of FuMO 2 Calais surface-search radars to detect Allied warships and transports. Co-located at the same site was the Luftwaffe "Igel" station of 9./Ln.Rgt. 53 (*Luftnachrichtenregiment*: Air Surveillance Regiment) with a pair of FuSE 65 Wurzberg-Riese air-search radars. This site was linked by radio to Pointe-du-Hoc and higher commands by teams from Funkmess-Kompanie 369, which had radio personnel at both Le Guay and Pointe-du-Hoc.

The autumn of 1943 saw extensive personnel changes at Pointe-du-Hoc. The Wehrmacht in Russia was so desperate for troops that nearly all formations in France were combed for personnel, and then replaced by older reservists or wounded veterans not suitable for combat duty in the east. Not only were many of the younger artillery crews sent off to Russia, but not enough replacements were provided to keep the battery at full strength, falling from an authorized strength of 146 to about 120 men in the autumn of 1943 and to about 85 men by the early summer of 1944. On October 22, 1943, three British warships appeared off Colleville at the eastern extreme of the battery's effective range. They were not engaged by the battery and when the battalion commander, Major Clemens Warlimont, angrily called Leutnant Ebeling and asked why he hadn't attacked them, he nonchalantly replied "I can't hit sparrows with these guns." Ebeling was unceremoniously sent to an artillery unit in Russia and his place was taken by the battery's assistant chief, Oberleutnant Brotkorb.

On December 15, 1943, there was another reorganization of German coastal defenses in lower Normandy due to the initiatives of field marshals Rommel and Rundstedt, who had been appointed by Hitler in the autumn of 1943 to reinvigorate defenses in France. Rundstedt insisted that greater unity of command be imposed on the coastal batteries. Up until this point, the Heer and Kriegsmarine had built their own coastal batteries independently due to their different conceptions about configuration and tactics. The army batteries were usually located away from the coast, relying on indirect fire; they used towed guns and the casemates were designed with rear doors so that the guns could be moved from inactive sectors to reinforce threatened sectors. Pointe-du-Hoc was an exception to the army's usual practice, and was located directly on the coast due to the advantages of the promontory. The Kriegsmarine's "warships of the dunes" used fixed pedestal mounts, often standard warship weapons, and were normally located on the shore to engage in direct-fire engagements with enemy warships. The Heer complained that the Kriegsmarine batteries were too vulnerable to enemy naval bombardment. The Kriegsmarine complained that the army batteries lacked proper fire control procedures and so were useless in engaging moving targets such as warships, which was their ostensible function. A Swedish coastal defense officer who visited the Normandy batteries after the war strongly favored the Kriegsmarine approach and noted the inadequate fire controls of the army batteries when engaging ships.

Regardless of this debate, Rundstedt won Hitler's support to apply a more unified command of the batteries. As a result, HKAA.832 was reorganized as HKAR.1260 (*Heeres-Küsten-Artillerie-Regiment*); the principal change was that the Kriegsmarine battery under construction at Longues-sur-Mer became the regiment's fourth battery and the Pointe-du-Hoc battery became 2./HKAR.1260. The fortified battery at Pointe-du-Hoc was redesignated as WN 75 (*Wiederstandsnest*: Resistance Nest) and became part of *Stützpunkt Pointe-du-Hoc* which included the small infantry post WN 76 located to the west.

The traditional German doctrine for repelling amphibious landings was to place a thin screen of defenses forward, to control the ports and major river estuaries, and to hold the main force behind the beach. When the enemy landings took place, the main forces could then move forward in a violent, mobile counterattack. This pattern was repeated time and time again in the Mediterranean theater at Sicily, Salerno, and Anzio. However, Rommel felt that this tactic was bankrupt due to overwhelming

Allied air and naval power and he insisted that the bulk of the forces be moved directly to the beach to stop the enemy landings at the water's edge on the first day of fighting. As a result, Rommel ordered units in the LXXXIV Corps sector in lower Normandy to begin shifting more of their forces directly to the beach. Pointe-du-Hoc was located on the section of the coast held by the III.Bataillon/Grenadier-Regiment 726 (III./GR.726) of the 716.Infanterie-Division. Its four companies were thinly stretched from Grandcamp to the beach at Colleville–Vierville, the latter sector better known as Omaha Beach, and on further west towards Pointe-du-Hoc. Since this battalion had no troops to spare, the Pointe-du-Hoc battery was gradually reinforced by a hodge-podge of other troops as they became available.

In March 1944, the 352.Infanterie-Division began taking over the defense of the Grandcamp sector, but GR.726 remained in place under the new division's command. The 1.Schwadron of Füsilier-Bataillon 352 was moved to Grandcamp where it was involved in laying barbed wire, beach obstructions, and mines along the coast including the shore area below the Pointe-du-Hoc in the weeks prior to D-Day. "Roller-mines" were placed along the cliffs; these were old French heavy artillery projectiles suspended over the cliff by cable with either an impact fuze to detonate when dropped, or a remote-detonation fuze that could be set off from the cliff-top. In May 1944, Werfer-Regiment 84 (*Werfer*: lit. "launcher"), an artillery multiple rocket launcher unit, was ordered forward from Rouen out of corps reserve and stationed on Omaha Beach in the St Laurent draw. However, a section of 15 troops from this unit was transferred to Pointe-du-Hoc on May 23, 1944, where they were deployed as machine-gun teams in fox-holes dug above the cliffs on both the eastern and western sides of the promontory, as a token gesture to move more of the defenses directly up to the coast. The battery officers thought that this was a waste of resources, as they felt that the cliffs offered an impregnable defense. Most of the battery's defenses were oriented southward, expecting that any attempt to take the strongpoint would come from the land side, and anti-glider obstacles were being added to the southward defenses as an Allied airborne assault was viewed as the main threat.

Initial Allied Plans

Grandcamp was located in the US Army sector of Operation *Neptune*, with the coast between Vierville and Colleville becoming Omaha Beach, and the area northwest of the Vire estuary later being added to the plans as Utah Beach. As a result, the problem of Pointe-du-Hoc was assigned to the US Army. By early 1944, the Operation *Neptune* plan had moved in the direction of using US airborne forces to seize the areas behind Utah Beach, so the mission to deal with Pointe-du-Hoc fell to the US Rangers.

The Rangers had been created in May 1942 as a counterpart to the widely admired British Commandos. Eisenhower felt that the Commando name should remain unique to the British special operations forces, so the US Army equivalents were called Rangers from Rogers' Rangers of the French-and-Indian War. The Ranger concept was not appreciated by senior army commanders, notably LtGen Lesley McNair, the chief of Army Ground Forces. McNair was the architect of the wartime army and preferred standardized unit organizations that could be tailored for the occasional special mission. He did not favor special forces units, fearing they would drain the regular infantry of the most highly motivated troops who could be more profitably used for the junior leadership ranks of the regular infantry. He was also concerned that special forces units would tend to create secondary missions to justify their existence. Regardless of his views, McNair gradually acquiesced to the formation of small numbers of Ranger units.

The 1st Ranger Battalion was raised in Scotland in June 1942 by calling for volunteers from US infantry units already in Britain. It was better known as "Darby's Rangers," after the battalion's founding commander, LtCol William Darby. A small number of Rangers took part in the ill-fated Dieppe raid in August 1942. The 1st Ranger Battalion was subsequently used in Allied amphibious operations in the Mediterranean theater, first at Arzew in Algeria during Operation *Torch* in November 1942, at Gela on Sicily during Operation *Husky* in July 1943, in Operationa *Shingle* at Salerno in September 1943 (along with the 3rd and 4th Rangers), and finally at Anzio in January 1944, where the battalion was later decimated. The first Ranger unit formed for the European Theater of Operations (ETO) was the Provisional 29th Ranger Battalion composed of volunteers from the 29th Division in December 1942. The battalion saw action alongside the Commandos on a number of small raids in the summer and autumn of 1943, and was used in a battalion-sized raid on Île-d'Quessant off the Breton coast in the summer of 1943. The battalion was disbanded in October 1943 and its troops re-absorbed into the 29th Division, which was earmarked to land at Omaha Beach.

The 2nd Ranger Battalion was formed in April 1943 at Camp Forrest, Tennessee, to create a regular Ranger battalion for the ETO. The battalion was led from June 1943 by 34-year-old Maj James Rudder. He had been commissioned into the Army reserves in 1932 after graduating from Texas A&M and was a teacher and football coach at a small Texas college until being called to active duty in 1941. The Ranger battalions had their own table of organization and were smaller and lighter than normal infantry battalions. Instead of the infantry battalion's three rifle companies and one weapons company, the Ranger battalion had six assault companies (A to F). In terms of battalion strength, a regular infantry battalion had 871 men versus the Ranger's 516 troops. The Rangers demanded aggressive, self-motivated soldiers in top physical shape and there were more than 2,000 volunteers for the unit, enduring high turn-overs until it was finally winnowed down to its core strength of about 550 troops. One of the young officers of the battalion, Lt James Eikner, explained the motivation of the Rangers: "These units accepted only volunteers; men were selected for their mental and physical stamina and their motivation to get the job done. Sometimes we were called a 'suicide group'. But not at all! We were simply spirited young people who took the view that if you were going to be a combat soldier, you may as well be the very best."

From the outset, the 2nd Rangers had been earmarked for Operation *Neptune*. In September 1943, the battalion went through the bug-infested Scout and Raiders School at Ft Pierce, Florida, to receive amphibious assault training, and departed for

The 2nd Rangers trained extensively on amphibious operations and cliff climbing in the months prior to D-Day. This is a landing exercise on the English coast in the spring of 1944, with the rocket-equipped LCA 722 evident in the background. (MHI)

Three of the 2nd Rangers' officers are seen here from a larger group portrait of the HQ company taken at Ft Dix, New Jersey, in 1943 before debarkation to Britain. From left to right are: communications officer Lt James Eikner; battalion commander LtCol James Rudder; and battalion medical officer Maj Walter "Doc" Block. (MHI)

Britain on November 11, 1943. The battalion was first stationed in Bude in Cornwall, where cliff-climbing exercises were conducted in conjunction with British Commandos; this training was not peculiar to the Pointe-du-Hoc mission, but was standard in all Ranger programs due to the prevalence of cliffs along much of the French coast. The final series of cliff-climbing exercises was conducted in the spring of 1944 at Swanage in Dorset, including the use of specialized equipment intended for the Pointe-du-Hoc mission. Although there were efforts to season the men by using them in commando raids on the French coast in early 1944, these never took place.

Planning for the attack on the Normandy coastal batteries was under the purview of Britain's Combined Operations Directorate, which was in charge of the Commandos as well as the Royal Navy landing craft flotillas used to deliver special operations troops. Combined Operations also fostered the development of much of the specialized equipment that the Rangers would use on D-Day. The specialized equipment was tested at "Westward Ho," the Combined Operations Experimental Establishment near Bideford in Devon. Much of the equipment was developed by the "Wheezers and Dodgers," the Department of Miscellaneous Weapons Development of the Admiralty. To surmount the cliffs rapidly, rocket-propelled grapnel hooks, based on existing rocket projectors, were designed to loft climbing ropes. The heavy configuration was adapted from the 2in rocket and "J-Projector" with a grapnel hook mounted in front, connected by a wire strap to a length of rope in nearby boxes. After considerable experimentation, the final configuration was to place six of these projectors on each Ranger LCA (Landing Craft, Assault). The first pair would launch ¾in ropes; the second pair launched rope with small wooden toggles tied in the rope at intervals to assist in climbing; the third pair launched a rope ladder. A lighter version was also developed from the Schermuly mortar with 1in rocket as used by coast-guard life-saving units, and the Rangers could carry these onto the beach should the main projectors fail. A somewhat more conventional approach was the use of the "Light Tubular Steel Ladder," configured in 16ft sections. Each LCA carried 110ft of the ladder, which would be assembled on the beach into greater lengths where needed. The Rangers also carried coils of rope to augment the rocket-fired ropes, and they were trained in the use of daggers to assist in climbing cliffs made from soft sediment.

The most elaborate cliff-scaling device was created by mounting 100ft extension ladders obtained from the London fire brigades on a DUKW amphibious truck. Extensible jacks were mounted on either side to stabilize the DUKW once the ladder was erected. To assist in the mission, the ladders were fitted with a pair of Lewis light machine-guns at the top to help clear the cliff-top of any opposition. The four Ladder-DUKWs assigned to the 2nd Rangers were named Swan 1–4.

While the initial training of the 2nd Rangers was underway, the 5th Ranger Battalion was formed at Camp Forrest to provide a second battalion for the D-Day missions. This battalion was formed of volunteers like the 2nd Rangers and departed for Scotland in March 1944 to complete training with the British Commandos. On D-Day, it was commanded by LtCol Max Schneider, former executive officer of the 2nd Rangers, and a veteran of Ranger operations in North Africa, Sicily, and Italy in 1942–43.

THE PLAN

Allied planners viewed the Pointe-du-Hoc battery as such a danger to Allied assault transports that the Navy moved the Omaha Beach "Transport Area," where the landing craft would be launched, further out to sea and beyond the range of the guns. Initial planning presumed that the key coastal batteries at Pointe-du-Hoc and Ouistreham would be eliminated from the ground by Commandos and Rangers in the pre-dawn darkness before the transports would congregate in the Transport Area, several hours before the main dawn landings. In February 1944, it was realized that this sequence would not be possible because the mine-sweeping flotillas would be in the vanguard of the main landing force. A separate minesweeping effort for the small special operations forces was impractical and so the Rangers would have to land in roughly the same time frame as the main force. This was a significant shift in plans, since it implied that the guns might still be active when the main landings occurred at H-Hour (0630hrs). As a result, the plans began to place more emphasis on the use of airpower not merely to "soften" the gun batteries, but to obliterate them. The Ranger raid was still included in the plan, as there was no assurance that the air attacks would eliminate the threat. Although it was not explicitly stated in the plan, a secondary reason for the Ranger mission to Pointe-du-Hoc was to provide some linkage on the right flank of the V Corps Omaha Beach landing to the VII Corps landing on Utah Beach.

In actuality, Allied intelligence exaggerated the threat posed by Pointe-du-Hoc and underestimated its vulnerability. The battery had little capability to engage targets in the dark, lacking naval plotting equipment. Allied intelligence did not know this, and planned for a worse-case scenario. The threat posed by the Longues-sur-Mer battery east of Omaha beach, which did have plotting equipment and the capability to engage naval targets, was largely ignored, as the battery was not completed until May 1944 and its technical features were not known by Allied intelligence. Pointe-du-Hoc had less capability to engage targets on Utah Beach for purely organizational and not technical reasons. The Vire River marked a German corps boundary and the Utah Beach area was well covered by coastal artillery from another regiment, as well as divisional artillery.

Under the final *Neptune* plan, the elimination of Pointe-du-Hoc was a three-step process: air power would be used to soften the position prior to D-Day, followed by heavy bombers and naval bombardment in the early morning hours of D-Day to

The challenge posed by the cliffs at Pointe-du-Hoc led to the use of a variety of specialized cliff-climbing aids developed by British Combined Operations. This photograph shows one of the LCAs used by the 2nd Rangers during exercises on the English coast in the spring of 1944, firing grapnel rockets from six "J-Projectors" mounted on the upper parts of the craft. (MHI)

prevent the battery from interfering with the first wave assault, and finally the Ranger raid would secure the battery. The raid was a two-battalion mission involving both the 2nd and 5th Rangers. A Provisional Ranger Group was created, led by the 2nd Rangers' commander, James Rudder, by now a lieutenant colonel. The two-battalion option provided the mission with greater tactical flexibility since there was much uncertainty about the magnitude of the challenge posed by Pointe-du-Hoc. Some officers felt that it was a suicide mission and that "Three old women with brooms could keep the Rangers from climbing that cliff." Rudder and the other senior Ranger commanders were flabbergasted when first told of the plans in the spring of 1944, and at first thought the plan was an elaborate joke. Yet the planners were convinced that the preliminary bombardment would substantially reduce the German defenses, that naval gunfire would keep those defenses in check, and that surprise and audacity would work in favor of the plan. The availability of a second battalion could cover the contingencies and if the initial assault by the 2nd Rangers failed, the 5th Rangers would land away from Pointe-du-Hoc, and then march to the site and attack it from the landward side.

Prelude to *Flashlamp*: Air Force Raids

Although the possibility of eliminating the coastal artillery batteries by concentrated air attack was considered, in 1943 it was not clear what resources would actually be available. The US Strategic Air Force in Europe (USSTAF) was dedicated to the use of the heavy bombers of the Eighth and Fifteenth Air Forces for strategic missions. In the spring of 1944, it was deeply committed to Operation *Pointblank*, a campaign to destroy the Luftwaffe prior to D-Day by daylight bombing raids against German aircraft plants, combined with the attrition of Luftwaffe fighter squadrons by the use of deep-penetration fighter escorts. The USSTAF commander, LtGen Carl Spaatz, was adamantly opposed to diverting the heavy bombers from these missions for use against tactical targets such as the coastal batteries. Eisenhower's deputy, Air Chief Marshal Arthur

Combined Operations developed a version of the DUKW amphibious truck fitted with extensible ladders borrowed from the London fire brigades, and one is seen here on trials. Although three of the four arrived safely at Pointe-du-Hoc, the shoreline was too torn up by the preliminary bombardment to provide the necessary footing for the vehicles, so they were not used. (Tank Museum)

Tedder, argued that bombing raids were ineffective against steel-reinforced concrete coastal artillery bunkers and would be valuable only if staged before the concrete had been set, or in a last-minute raid to disrupt the operation of the battery. Regardless of these objections, the *Neptune* planners wanted air attacks to "soften" the coastal batteries.

The attack on the coastal batteries was complicated by the fact that if the bombing raids concentrated on the lower Normandy sites, then the Germans would no doubt deduce the location of Operation *Neptune*. So the bombing plan presumed that three missions would be flown against sites in upper Normandy and the Pas-de-Calais for every mission flown against coastal batteries in lower Normandy. To placate Spaatz and avoid the diversion of heavy bombers, the burden of the missions fell on the newly arrived medium bombers of the Ninth Air Force. The heavy bombers of both the US Army Air Forces (USAAF) and Royal Air Force (RAF) would not be brought to bear until the final raids in the days immediately preceding D-Day, codenamed Operation *Flashlamp*, based on Tedder's objections. *Flashlamp* paid special attention to ten coastal batteries, of which four were singled out as posing a special hazard to the landing force: Pointe-du-Hoc, Houlgate, Villerville, and Ouistreham.

The first major raid on Pointe-du-Hoc by A-20 Havocs of the 409th and 416th Bomb Groups on the evening of April 25 crippled the battery and forced the evacuation of the guns to a more secure location more than a mile from the battery positions. Smoke can be seen rising from Pointe-du-Hoc, visible below the lead aircraft of this formation. (Library of Congress)

The Ninth Air Force operation against the coastal batteries began on April 13, 1944. The Pointe-du-Hoc battery was hit for the first time in the early evening of April 25, 1944, while many of the troops were queuing up for supper at the canteen in the Guelinel farm. Two waves of A-20 Havoc bombers of the 409th and 416th Bomb Groups (BG) began their attacks at 1659hrs, dropping about 40 tons of bombs. The crews assessed their accuracy as generally good. From the German perspective, the attack was both accurate and devastating. The bombs destroyed two of the six kettle emplacements and one of the six guns, and damaged two other guns. A number of other buildings were hit, although personnel casualties were surprisingly light with only two dead, one severely wounded, and two lightly wounded.

The heavy damage inflicted on the guns forced the battery to withdraw them to a safer location. From nightfall on April 25 through the night of April 26, the gun crews moved the five surviving guns to a sunken lane along a tree-line about

APRIL 25–JUNE 6
1944

Ninth Air Force bombing campaign against Pointe-du-Hoc

Bomber Attacks against Pointe-du-Hoc

Date	Attack Time	Unit	Aircraft	Bomb tonnage
Apr 25	1659	416 BG	35 (2)* A-20	33.75
Apr 25	1731	409 BG	16 (4) A-20	16
May 13	1139	322 BG	33 (2) B-26	69
May 22	1928	323 BG	29 (3) B-26	56
Jun 4	1510	416 BG	43 A-20	50.5
Jun 4	1522	409 BG	42 A-20	51
Jun 5	0921	379 BG	35 B-17	104.25
Jun 6	0446	8 Group (RAF)	9 (2) Mosquito	2.5 (illumination)
Jun 6	0450–0503	5 Group (RAF)	108 (7) Lancaster	634.8
Jun 6	0630	391 BG	9 (8) B-26	16

*Data in parentheses indicate aircraft which sortied but aborted

0.8 miles south, outside of the battery site. The sixth destroyed gun was moved away from the emplacement but the wreckage was left within the battery site. Since the battery's principal mission was to defend the port of Grandcamp and the Vire estuary, all five guns were eventually placed in field positions pointing west, and the guns were covered with camouflage nets to hide them from Allied observation. The battery was never able to get replacement parts to make the two damaged guns functional. In other words, this modest raid had effectively eliminated half the battery and forced the Germans to evacuate the site to an unprotected location, separating the guns from their fire control bunker, fortified ammunition bunkers and personnel shelters. While half the guns could still be employed, they would be far more vulnerable to counter-battery fire or air attack, have restricted access to ammunition, and have significantly more difficulty engaging targets accurately.

To confuse Allied intelligence and to discourage them from hunting for the hidden guns, the battery located some telegraph poles, which were set up in the emplacements with wooden supports to resemble the missing guns, while the gun pits remained covered under camouflage nets. André Farina, a member of the local French *Centurie* resistance cell, saw the re-positioned guns, which were well outside the battery's restricted perimeter. He passed this information to the head of his cell, Jean Marion, who attempted to inform London by the standard means of a carrier pigeon. However, the 352.Infanterie-Division had been warned about the French use of carrier pigeons and in late March 1944 had established anti-pigeon patrols along the coast by arming the local troops with shotguns. German sources state that this particular pigeon was one of those that were shot down. In total, 27 pigeons were shot down from March 20 to May 27, 1944, according to division records.

Allied intelligence was largely unaware of the success of April 25 raid. Aerial reconnaissance aircraft photographed the site and noted several near misses on the gun pits. However, the reconstructed camouflage nets over the gun pits and the telephone-pole ruse led Allied photo interpreters to believe that five of the six gun pits were still occupied. The sixth pit was no longer operational, as it was absorbed into the construction of one of the new gun casemates. The battery was strafed by P-47 Thunderbolts on May 21, but the 37mm Flak responded and one fighter limped away, trailing smoke. The increased intensity of the air attacks led Flak-Sturm-Regiment 1 to move one of its 88mm guns from the highway positions south of the coast to the battery site, and it was positioned near the west Flak bunker.

The next attack by 33 B-26 Marauder medium bombers of the 322nd BG hit Pointe-du-Hoc on the early afternoon of May 13. Later photo reconnaissance suggested that no additional damage had been caused to the guns, but once again this was due to the battery crews hastily reconstructing the camouflage nets over the gun pits, hiding any damage. German accounts indicate that the raid largely crushed the communication trenches running between the main sites, but caused no casualties. The May 13 mission, however, had some consequence for the eventual fighting on Pointe-du-Hoc. A number of the heavy bombs fell in the minefield on the south side of the position, leading to sympathetic detonations of neighboring mines that partially cleared the minefield. On May 22, 29 B-26 Marauders of the 323rd BG hit Pointe-du-Hoc in the early evening. The post-strike assessment was fair to poor; German accounts indicate that one more gun pit was destroyed. The Guelinel farm that housed the battery's horses and canteen was largely destroyed in this attack and the Organization Todt ceased all construction work at the site due to the hazard. The final pre-D-Day medium bomber raid was conducted again by another joint mission of the 416th and 409th BG in the late afternoon of June 4, with 85 A-20 Havocs dropping a hundred tons of bombs, with results judged to be fair to good.

It was now the turn of the heavy bombers and Operation *Flashlamp*. On the morning of June 5, 35 B-17 bombers of the 379th BG dropped over a hundred tons of bombs on Pointe-du-Hoc, including about 10 tons of special armor-piercing (SAP) bombs to deal with the reinforced bunkers. The attack was assessed to have delivered at least 50 bombs into the battery site, with two guns "probably destroyed." German reports indicate that one more gun pit was destroyed, along with at least one ammunition bunker. Three personnel bunkers had received direct hits, yet suffered only insignificant damage due to the soundness of their design and construction. The most common type of bomb used in the air attacks was the 500lb high-explosive bomb, and this was not sufficient to penetrate the "bomb-proof" personnel bunkers, which were hardened to withstand 1,000lb bombs.

Prior to D-Day, Pointe-du-Hoc had been attacked by 380 tons of bombs, more than 10 tons per acre. In combination with the D-Day air raids, Pointe-du-Hoc was more heavily bombed than any other site in Normandy. Two more attacks were planned to take place on the morning of D-Day, a massive strike by RAF heavy bombers followed by a US medium bomber strike to prevent any recovery of the battery. Even before these raids, the Pointe-du-Hoc battery was badly torn up, with most of the communication trenches buried, three gun pits destroyed and the remaining two damaged, both gun casemates intact but damaged, and many of the field telephone lines disrupted. The bombing had gradually obliterated the roads, making it very difficult to shift ammunition remaining in the bunkers to the guns located away from the battery site. Some of the ammunition had been removed to dumps in the St Lô area for safe-keeping. While the combat effectiveness of the Pointe-du-Hoc battery had been substantially degraded, this was not apparent to Allied intelligence. The last full-scale intelligence interpretation from aerial photographs on May 29 concluded that five of the six gun pits were occupied, suggesting that five guns were still operational; the location of the sixth gun was unknown but it might be concealed at the site.

The neighboring radar site, *Stützpunkt Le Guay*, did not suffer the heavy attacks directed against Pointe-du-Hoc. This was largely due to the Allied belief that radar sites were resistant to bombing attack and that the antennas were relatively easy to repair. So Allied planners waited until the last few weeks before D-Day before starting the anti-radar campaign. As in the case of the coastal battery attacks, the radar attacks were staged in greater numbers on the upper Normandy and Pas-de-Calais coast than on the lower Normandy coast to continue to maintain the ruse that

The former Guelinel farm on Pointe-du-Hoc had been used as the canteen, barracks, and stables for the battery, but it was thoroughly destroyed in the pre-invasion bombing, as seen here. (MHI)

RANGER ASSAULT ON POINTE-DU-HOC, D-DAY, JUNE 6, 1944

The area detailed on this map is 750m wide and 1243m deep.

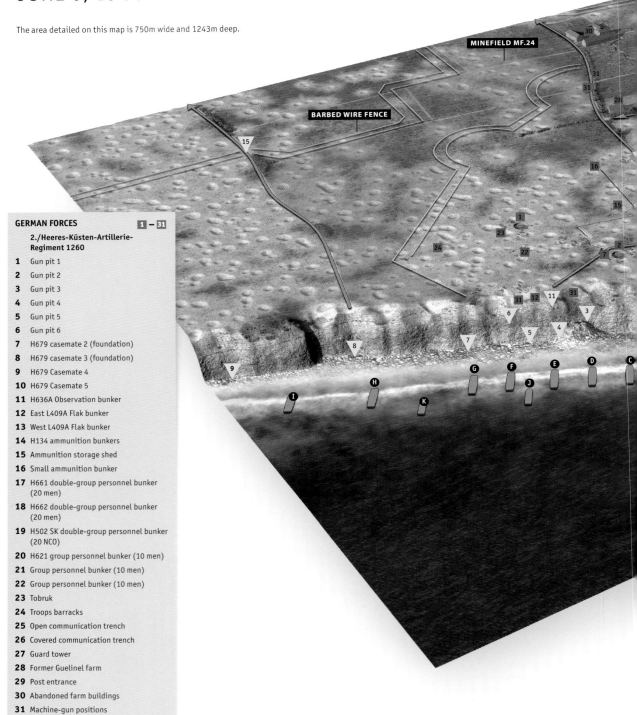

MINEFIELD MF.24

BARBED WIRE FENCE

GERMAN FORCES   `1` – `31`

2./Heeres-Küsten-Artillerie-Regiment 1260

1   Gun pit 1
2   Gun pit 2
3   Gun pit 3
4   Gun pit 4
5   Gun pit 5
6   Gun pit 6
7   H679 casemate 2 (foundation)
8   H679 casemate 3 (foundation)
9   H679 Casemate 4
10   H679 Casemate 5
11   H636A Observation bunker
12   East L409A Flak bunker
13   West L409A Flak bunker
14   H134 ammunition bunkers
15   Ammunition storage shed
16   Small ammunition bunker
17   H661 double-group personnel bunker (20 men)
18   H662 double-group personnel bunker (20 men)
19   H502 SK double-group personnel bunker (20 NCO)
20   H621 group personnel bunker (10 men)
21   Group personnel bunker (10 men)
22   Group personnel bunker (10 men)
23   Tobruk
24   Troops barracks
25   Open communication trench
26   Covered communication trench
27   Guard tower
28   Former Guelinel farm
29   Post entrance
30   Abandoned farm buildings
31   Machine-gun positions

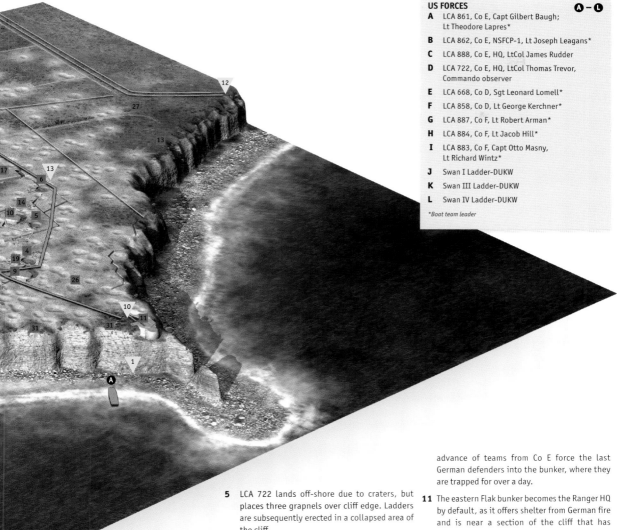

US FORCES **Ⓐ – Ⓛ**

A LCA 861, Co E, Capt Gilbert Baugh;
Lt Theodore Lapres*

B LCA 862, Co E, NSFCP-1, Lt Joseph Leagans*

C LCA 888, Co E, HQ, LtCol James Rudder

D LCA 722, Co E, HQ, LtCol Thomas Trevor,
Commando observer

E LCA 668, Co D, Sgt Leonard Lomell*

F LCA 858, Co D, Lt George Kerchner*

G LCA 887, Co F, Lt Robert Arman*

H LCA 884, Co F, Lt Jacob Hill*

I LCA 883, Co F, Capt Otto Masny,
Lt Richard Wintz*

J Swan I Ladder-DUKW

K Swan III Ladder-DUKW

L Swan IV Ladder-DUKW

*Boat team leader

ACTIONS

1 Grapnel rockets onboard LCA 861 fail to reach the cliff edge; two hand-rockets launched. Team suffers two casualties to hand-grenades; large roller-mine exploded overhead.

2 Two grapnel rockets from LCA 862 find purchase; two men wounded by grenades, two by machine-gun fire from the east.

3 Rudder's LCA 888 is first to arrive. All grapnel rockets fail to reach the cliff edge, but a large section of collapsed cliff and spoil at the bottom permit the use of ladders.

4 Two grapnel rockets from LCA 722 reach the cliff edge. This craft contains the Force's main SCR-284 radio and a 60mm mortar team.

5 LCA 722 lands off-shore due to craters, but places three grapnels over cliff edge. Ladders are subsequently erected in a collapsed area of the cliff.

6 Only one grapnel rocket from LCA 858 reaches top of cliff, but team climbs quickly.

7 After only one of the forward grapnel rockets manages to reach the cliff edge, LCA 887 beaches and Sgt John Cripps removes J-Projectors to shore and fires them by hand.

8 LCA 884 gets four ropes over the cliff, but is hit by considerable small-arms fire, suffering three casualties on the beach. Since the cliff top is too vulnerable to continuing small-arms fire, team heads left and uses ropes from neighboring LCA 883.

9 LCA 883 is only craft to get all six ropes over the cliff edge. It is sheltered by a protruding cliff, avoiding machine-gun fire coming from a German position to the left.

10 Forward observation post is the scene of the most intense German resistance, but the advance of teams from Co E force the last German defenders into the bunker, where they are trapped for over a day.

11 The eastern Flak bunker becomes the Ranger HQ by default, as it offers shelter from German fire and is near a section of the cliff that has collapsed, providing access by ladder and rope.

12 The western Flak bunker is one of the few German positions to remain relatively unscathed by the *Flashlamp* raid, and its intact 20mm gun makes it a rallying point for German troops on the west side of the strongpoint.

13 The Co D teams were supposed to land on the west side of Pointe-du-Hoc, and so have the farthest to traverse to locate their assigned guns. After finding the gun pits empty, they head to the strongpoint exit where they meet a Co E team.

14 Co E quarantines the observation bunker, and then a team checks its assigned gun pits and, after discovering them empty, heads to the rallying point and the Grandcamp road beyond.

15 Co F lands much further to the left than intended, and a team heads to Grandcamp road from the area outside the strongpoint perimeter.

the Allied landings would come in those areas. On May 10, 1944, the Allied tactical air forces started their campaign to knock out German radar sites, beginning with the large early-warning radars which would take the longest time to repair, and then working their way down to the small tactical coastal radars. An initial raid on *Stützpunkt Le Guay* by four P-47 Thunderbolts of the Ninth Tactical Air Force on May 21 was ineffective. These sites presented a difficult target for fighter-bombers, as the attacks had to be pressed home very close to ensure a high probability of hitting the antennas or the supporting generators and control buildings. Furthermore, the German positions were well defended with *Stützpunkt Le Guay* having no fewer than four 20mm Flak cannon with additional Flak batteries in the area south of the coast along the main Cherbourg highway. A more determined attack with rockets and bombs was made by 20 fighter-bombers on May 23, with two of the radar antennas hit and damage estimated at 20 percent by the German report. Two more attacks took place on May 24 and May 30, but were not especially effective – an RAF Typhoon IB of 197 Squadron was shot down by 20mm Flak on the May 24 raid. As a result, prior to D-Day the "Imme" and "Igel" radar stations were damaged but still functional.

The Raiding Force

The initial assault on Beach Charlie was assigned to the 2nd Rangers, in two groups. The main raid against Pointe-du-Hoc was assigned to Ranger Force A consisting of Assault Cos D, E, and F. Force B, consisting of C/2nd Rangers, had the separate mission of landing on the right side of the 116th Regimental Combat Team (RCT) near the Vierville draw, and advancing overland along the top of the bluffs to assault the German strongpoints on the Point-et-Raz-de-la-Percée, which posed a dangerous threat of enfilade fire against the eastern side of Omaha Beach. It would then continue to march overland to Pointe-du-Hoc, eliminating the radar station at Le Guay in the

A group of Rangers inside an LCA in port before heading out to the landing ships on June 4. Most of the photos of the LCA in Weymouth and Portsmouth harbors show Force C, as the rocket-grapnel launchers on the Force A LCA were considered secret. (NARA)

Teams from the 5th Rangers and the 507 LCA Flotilla are loaded aboard LSI(S)-3 *Prince Baudoin* on June 4 off the English coast.

process. The 116th RCT consisted of the 116th Infantry Regiment of the 29th Division, along with its supporting units such as the 743rd Tank Battalion, and was commanded by Col Charles Canham; it was initially under the command of the 1st Infantry Division.

If the initial assault on Pointe-du-Hoc succeeded, Force A would be followed by LtCol Max Schneider's Force C, which consisted of the 5th Rangers, along with the remaining Cos A and B from 2nd Rangers. If the initial landing against Pointe-du-Hoc failed, the 5th Rangers would land on Beach Dog Green near the Vierville draw and then advance overland to attack Pointe-du-Hoc. To provide additional fire support for the Provisional Ranger Group, a Cannon Platoon was added to the 2nd Rangers HQ company in early 1944, patterned after a similar unit belonging to Darby's Rangers in Italy. This platoon consisted of four M3 75mm Gun Motor Carriages (GMCs), an obsolete halftrack tank-destroyer fitted with a 75mm gun, and a pair of .50cal machine-guns. These were carried on Landing Craft, Tank (LCT) vessels and were part of Force C.

Force A would be delivered to the cliffs at the base of Pointe-du-Hoc by ten LCA with Co D landing on the western side of the point and Cos E and F on the eastern side. The individual Rangers in Force A were lightly equipped, typically with the standard M1 rifle, 128 rounds of ammunition, and six grenades. The best climbers in each team were dubbed "top monkeys" and would be the first up the ropes; they were armed only with pistols and carbines. Support weapons were limited to four Browning Automatic Rifles (BARs) and two 60mm mortars; two 81mm mortars were to be brought in on the two supply craft. The Force A Rangers landed without the usual packs, which were carried on the supply craft, but some did wear the special assault vest that permitted additional gear to be carried. Besides the Rangers, the initial assault group was accompanied by Naval Shore Fire Control Party-1 (NSFCP-1) and an Army forward observer team from the 293rd Joint Assault Signal Company to direct gunfire support.

The naval element of attack, designated Assault Group O-4, was provided by British Combined Operations and consisted principally of Royal Navy craft and ships under the leadership of Cdr S. H. Dennis, RN. The mother-ships for the landing craft were Landing Ship, Infantry (LSI): the LSI(H) of Force A were converted British Channel steamers while the LSI(S) were converted Belgian cross-Channel ferries. Each LSI carried an LCA flotilla numbering six to eight LCA. The LCA could carry up to 32 men, but in Force A the average was closer to 22 troops due to the additional weight of the rocket-grapnel projectors and other equipment. The crew of each LCA was four sailors. They were typically armed with at least one Lewis gun.

Each landing force was assigned an accompanying Fairmile motor launch (ML), which provided navigation to steer the flotillas to their destinations. The two flotillas of Force A were accompanied by two Landing Craft Support, Medium – LCS(M) – which were converted LCA used as a fire support craft with additional heavy machine-guns and smoke mortars. In addition, both forces were supported by LCTs to carry vehicles; Force A had its own LCT while Force C relied on two LCTs of the 116th RCT.

There was an unexpected command change among the Rangers on the evening of June 5 before the flotillas departed Weymouth harbor for Normandy. As Rudder was in charge of the Ranger Group, command of Force A was handed over to Maj Cleveland Lytle, the Co A commander. That evening, several officers got together on the *Ben My Chree* to celebrate Joseph Rafferty's promotion to captain as the new commander of Co A. Some whiskey was passed around and Lytle got drunk. He began denouncing the raid as a suicide mission. The battalion medical officer, Capt Walter "Doc" Block, tried to restrain him, and Lytle punched the popular and respected officer. In the meantime, Rudder had been informed of the fracas, and walked over from the USS *Ancon* command ship where he was stationed. Rudder was infuriated and relieved Lytle on the spot; Lytle was transferred to the 90th Division where he later proved to be a brave and capable officer. Rudder felt that he had no choice but to take over command of Force A, as no other officer had been briefed on the complete details of the mission. This

2nd Ranger Battalion

	Commanding Officer	Executive Officer	Platoon Leaders
HQ	LtCol James Earl Rudder	Maj George Williams	
HQ Co	Capt James Wikner	Capt Frederick Wilkin	Lt J. Eikner, Lt C. Epperson, Lt W. Heaney, Lt J. McCullers, Lt E. Vermeer, Lt F. Kennard
Co A	Capt Joseph Rafferty		Lt Robert Edlin, Lt Stanley White
Co B	Capt Edgar Arnold		Lt Robert Brice, Lt Robert Fitzsimmons
Co C	Capt Ralph Goranson		Lt William Moody, Lt Sidney Salomon
Co D	Capt Harold Slater		Lt Morton McBride, Lt George Kirchner
Co E	Capt Gilbert Baugh		Lt Theodore Lapres, Lt Joseph Leagans

5th Ranger Battalion

	Commanding Officer	Executive Officer	Platoon Leaders
HQ	LtCol Max Schneider	Maj Richard Sullivan	
HQ Co	Capt John Raaen	Lt Howard Van Riper	Lt L. Gombosi, Lt Q. Knollenberg, Lt R. Nee, Lt J. Snyder
Co A	Capt Charles Parker		Lt Aloysius Wybroski, Lt Stanley Zelepsky
Co B	Capt George Whittington		Lt Bernard Pepper, Lt Matthew Gregory
Co C	Capt Wilmer Wise		Lt John Revile, Lt Jay Mehaffey
Co D	Capt Edward Luther		Lt Rayford Dendy, Lt Dee Anderson
Co E	Capt William Runge		Lt Frank Zidjunas, Lt William Mulligan

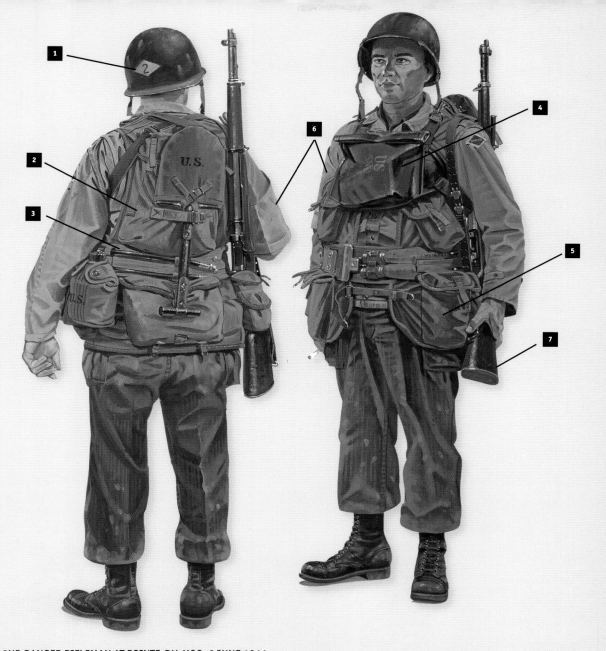

2ND RANGER RIFLEMAN AT POINTE-DU-HOC, 6 JUNE 1944

Aside from the Ranger insignia (1) painted on the back of the helmet, the Ranger troops assaulting Pointe-du-Hoc were equipped much the same as other US Army infantry of the assault waves on D-Day. One of the distinctive items issued to the assault waves was the "Assault Vest" (2), a multi-pocketed canvas vest that was worn in place of the usual webbing with separate musette bag and pouches. Instead, supplies were carried inside the assorted pockets and pouches (5) that were part of the vest. Another item widely issued for D-Day was the US Navy M-1926 life preserver belt which could be inflated using two compressed air cartridges near the front of the belt. Since there was concern that the Germans might use chemical weapons to repulse the landings, troops were issued with the M5 Assault Gas Mask which was contained in a waterproof M7 carrier covered in black neoprene (4) and worn on the chest. To detect the presence of gas, troops wore the British-made Gas Detector Sleeve (6) which was covered with a chemical-sensitive yellow-green paint that turned pink in the presence of chemical weapons. Both of these items tended to be discarded quickly after landing, as was the life preserver belt. The majority of Rangers at Pointe-du-Hoc were armed with the standard M1 "Garand" rifle (7).

Combined Operations Landing Force, Beach Charlie, D-Day

Ranger Force A				
Ship	Flotilla	LCA	Troops	Units
ML 304				Fairmile navigation launch
LCT 413				Ladder-DUKWs
LSI(H)-1 *Ben My Chree*	520 LCA Flotilla	6 LCA	112	Co F, Co E (-), Bn. HQ 2nd Ranger Battalion, 58th Armored Field Battalion (AFAB) Det.
LSI(H)-2 *Amsterdam*	522 LCA Flotilla	6 LCA	105	Co D, Co E (-), Bn. HQ 2nd Ranger Battalion, NSFCP-1
Ranger Force B/C				
ML 163				Fairmile navigation launch
LSI(S)-1 *Prince Charles*	501 LCA Flotilla	8 LCA	262	Cos A, B, C, HQ 2nd Ranger Battalion, NSFCP-2, 58th AFAB Det
LSI(S)-2 *Prince Leopold*	504 LCA Flotilla	7 LCA	244	Co A, Co F, HQ 5th Ranger Battalion
LSI(S)-3 *Prince Baudoin*	507 LCA Flotilla	7 LCA	246	Co C, Co D, Co F, HQ 5th Ranger Battalion

was opposed by both MajGen C. Huebner of the 1st Division, in command of Omaha Beach, and LtGen Omar Bradley, commander of US First Army, but both acquiesced to Rudder's decision. Rudder remained on the flotilla command ship LSI *Prince Charles* during transit to France, then at 0400hrs on D-Day he transferred to the *Ben My Chree*. This would have unfortunate consequences during the mission, as it left no officer aboard the command ships to coordinate support for the Rangers.

Only two casemates for the guns were finished, but they were never occupied. This is the westernmost of the two casemates, seen a few weeks after D-Day. (NARA)

Operation *Flashlamp*

Around midnight on June 5/6, German higher headquarters began to receive a stream of messages about increased Allied air and sea activity, and eventually about parachute drops around the Vire and Orne river estuaries on the Normandy coast. The coastal defenses were placed on full alert.

The first US troops to land at Pointe-du-Hoc were not in fact the Rangers. Around 0105hrs, a C-47 of the 96th Troop Carrier Squadron carrying a stick of paratroopers from Co I, 506th Parachute Infantry Regiment, 101st Airborne Division, was hit by Flak and went down off the coast of Pointe-du-Hoc. Before the plane crashed, at least four paratroopers got out. The jumpmaster, Lt Floyd Johnston, and Sgt Neil Christensen landed on Pointe-du-Hoc and both were captured after a short firefight; Johnston later escaped. Two other paratroopers, Sgt Raymond Crouch and Pvt Leonard Goodgall, landed on the shoreline under the promontory and remained there until dawn, when they joined up with the Rangers.

Operation *Flashlamp* commenced around 0445hrs in the pre-dawn twilight. A radar-equipped Mosquito IX flown by FltLt Gordon from 105 Squadron, 8 (Pathfinder) Group, began the attack with the dropping of red illumination flares; an accompanying Mosquito was unable to drop its markers. As these aircraft exited, three more Mosquitoes from 109 Squadron dropped green markers from altitudes of 30,000 and 18,000ft. Cloud cover that night varied, but was estimated about 5/10th cover. The bright markers provided the aiming point for the subsequent waves of Lancaster bombers. French farmers in the neighboring villages recalled that the "sky was on fire" as the brilliant markers cascaded down through the low clouds.

Within moments, the first stream of Lancaster bombers flew over Pointe-du-Hoc. The Lancasters of 9 Squadron started the bomb runs at 0453hrs at altitudes ranging from 6,500 to 8,500ft. The crews able to observe the ground described the bombing as accurate and well concentrated. In total, some eight Lancaster squadrons from 5 Group totaling 115 aircraft, along with four Mosquitos, bombed Pointe-du-Hoc for about a half hour, showering the site with 634.8 tons of bombs, over 20 tons per acre.

The effects of the bombing on the ground were devastating. The German defenders were already in the bunkers due to alert warnings, and the bunkers were actually quite resistant to bombs. However, the enormous volume of high explosives smashed up virtually everything but the bomb-proof shelters. Few trenches or roads escaped, and the entrances to many of the personnel shelters and ammunition bunkers were buried. The number of German casualties in the raid was never recorded; many of the survivors were deafened from punctured eardrums or other concussion injuries. The air raid had a debilitating effect on the morale of the survivors. The fire control team in the bunker at the tip of the promontory received a message that the gun crews stationed back away from the main position had located a farmer's wine cellar and had gotten thoroughly drunk. One veteran interviewed years later recalled that his shell-shocked gun crew simply said "screw this" and walked away from their position. The number of German troops still located in the

This sight is what the Rangers discovered when they reached the Pointe-du-Hoc gun pits. The fake telegraph-pole guns were disguised under wooden frames and camouflage net, all of which were knocked down during the pre-dawn Operation *Flashlamp* raid.

In an LCA in Weymouth harbor on June 4, we see troops of E/5th Rangers, including Sgt Sandy Martin (upper left), Sgt Joseph Markowitz (upper right), Cpl John Loshavio (lower right), and Pvt Frank Lockwood (lower left). (NARA)

The Rangers were landed aboard Royal Navy LCAs. LCA 1377 was part of the 507 LCA Flotilla from LSI(S)-3 *Prince Baudoin* landing a team from the 5th Rangers HQ headed by Capt John Raaen on Dog Green Beach. As can be seen, the LCA from Force B lacked the grapnel launchers fitted on the LCA of Force A. (NARA)

strongpoint after the air raid included the fire control party in the command bunker, most of the machine-gun crews from Werfer-Regiment 84 along the cliff edge, the anti-aircraft bunker on the west side of the position, which had escaped serious damage, and scattered groups of troops digging their way out from the bunkers. There were a few dozen German troops still active on Pointe-du-Hoc by the time dawn arrived, but many had abandoned the site, or had been buried or killed. There were also a number of construction workers on the site, including some Italian prisoners-of-war.

The attacking RAF bombers did not escape unscathed. In the early morning hours of D-Day, I./Schnellkampfgeschwader 10, a ground-attack "fast bomber

The Pointe-du-Hoc battery was struck in the pre-dawn hours by Lancaster bombers of the RAF's 5 Group as part of Operation *Flashlamp*, as seen in this illustration. The bombing runs were conducted at altitudes of 8,000–10,000 feet, and the target was periodically obscured by cloud cover. (Author)

wing" with Fw-190 fighter-bombers, was alerted to intercept Allied transports that were dropping paratroopers near Carentan. The 3.Staffel (a *Staffel* was equivalent to an Allied squadron) led by Hauptmann Eberspächer finally got airborne from Evreux airfield two hours late with four fighters, and was instructed to head for the coast and report on the situation. In the dim early morning light, the four fighters encountered the bomber stream from 5 Group as it was finishing its bomb-run over Pointe-du-Hoc. Eberspächer led the attack, claiming two Lancasters over Isigny and another over Carentan; another fighter claimed a Lancaster over Carentan. The air battles took place around 0501 to 0504hrs and were the first aerial engagements of D-Day. The German claims of four Lancasters were only slightly overstated; actual losses were two Lancasters from 97 Squadron and one Lancaster from 50 Squadron; three other Lancasters were damaged by Flak or fighters, but returned to base.

To further savage the strongpoint, Pointe-du-Hoc was listed as Target No. 1 for the US Navy's Bombardment Force C, which included the battleships USS *Texas* and *Arkansas* as well as a number of cruisers and destroyers. At 0550hrs, USS *Texas*, flagship of Rear Adm C. F. Bryant, began pounding the strongpoint with its 14in guns, firing some 250 rounds. One of the spotter planes from *Texas* orbited over Pointe-du-Hoc to call in artillery corrections. One of the most evident effects of its bombardment was to knock down a large chunk of the cliff immediately below the eastern Flak bunker; this would figure in subsequent developments. Also, the bombardment largely ended the threat of the roller-mines that had been hung along the cliff, as most were dislodged. The destroyer USS *Satterlee* attacked known pillboxes on the western side of Pointe-du-Hoc while HMS *Talybont* attacked the *Stützpunkt Le Guay* radar station and the defensive positions to the east of Pointe-du-Hoc. USS *Thompson* was assigned to bombard WN 74 at the tip of Pointe-et-Raz-de-Percée. The naval bombardment lifted at H-5, 0625hrs, in anticipation of the arrival of the Rangers at H-Hour. In the wake of this bombardment, the final but delayed air attack of Operation *Flashlamp* took place after 0630hrs, when nine B-26 bombers of the 391st BG arrived overhead and dropped another 16 tons of bombs on the strongpoint.

SEPTEMBER 29
1944

**0445hrs:
Start of Operation
*Flashlamp***

JUNE 6
1944

**0550–0625hrs:
Naval bombardment
of Pointe-du-Hoc**

THE RAID

The convoy from Weymouth arrived off Normandy around 0250hrs and the LCAs were lowered into the water from the LSI; the Force A Rangers took their place in the craft in the dark around 0400hrs. The water off Normandy was extremely choppy after the previous day's storm, and as the craft wallowed in the high seas the small vessels began to take on water and many Rangers became seasick. By 0430hrs, the craft had been joined by the two accompanying LCS(M) fire support craft and the two flotillas headed to shore. The run to the beach took two hours due to the sea state and the slow speed of the overweight LCAs. Around 0515hrs one of the supply LCAs sank, followed several minutes later by the second because of the high seas and the overloaded state of the craft. Around 0530hrs, LCA 860 carrying Capt Harold Slater and 20 troops from Co D swamped and sank; the troops were not rescued for several hours and suffered badly from exposure.

Leading the flotilla was Fairmile Motor Launch (ML) 304 commanded by Lt Colin Beever, RN Volunteer Reserve (RNVR). In the dark, the initial navigation was conducted using the Q.H. 2 "Tree" radio navigation set, which relied on cross bearings from transmitters in Britain and offered an accuracy of about 50 yards. The motor launch also had a Type 970 radar, but this was not helpful in providing directions against a shoreline that was featureless on a radar scope.

As dawn slowly arose, the coastline became evident, but the heavy bombardment and smoke made it difficult to locate landmarks with any precision. About 0530hrs, both the radar and Q.H. 2 had failed due to a faulty power supply. Beever had expected that Pointe-du-Hoc would be obvious due to the firing cannon, but he had a hard time distinguishing the Pointe-du-Hoc promontory from Pointe-et-Raz-de-la-Percée, which look very similar at sea-level. Around 0600hrs, while still about 3 miles from shore, Beever changed course to port and began heading for Pointe-et-Raz-de-la-Percée, mistaking it for Pointe-du-Hoc. Around 0540 and 4,000 yards from shore, LCT-46 received the codeword "Splash" and disgorged its four DUKWs into the water and they joined the LCA flotilla. By now, Rudder was convinced that the motor launch was leading them in the wrong direction and once they were about 1,000 yards from the point, he ordered the coxswain on LCA 888 to swing west. Beever by now recognized his mistake, as he could not see any evidence of the distinctive gun casemates on the point. The flotilla turned 160 degrees to starboard to reach the original point. By now, the small craft were within range of machine-guns on the cliffs above, and faced a 3-mile journey at slow speed under the cliffs. The commander of the destroyer HMS *Talybont*, LtCdr Baines, thought that the slow crawl to Pointe-du-Hoc along the cliffs "was suicidal."

Beever later wrote that during the final approach parallel to the cliffs his launch encountered only light machine-gun fire, which his crew countered with 20mm Oerlikon fire. However, the craft further behind in trail received more fire, including some bursts from a 20mm Flak gun. The sharp turn and the rough conditions swamped LCS(M) 91 and the craft began go down at the bow. It was hit repeatedly from a German machine-gun nest on the cliff, which was suppressed by machine-gun and mortar fire from the craft. In the meantime, LCS(M) 102 suffered the same fate, with the forepeak flooding and the mortar-well cover caving in, leaving the craft dead in the water. The rough water near the shore left most of the Rangers soaked, and many spent the final minutes of the approach using their helmets to bail water to prevent their craft from sinking. Baines onboard *Talybont* continued to shepherd the flotillas towards Pointe-du-Hoc, and when he saw machine-gun strikes in the water near the DUKWs, he brought his destroyer closer to shore and tried to engage the hidden German machine-gun nests with 4in guns and 2-pdr pom-pom anti-aircraft guns. Nevertheless, machine-gun fire hit DUKW *Swan-II* and disabled the engine, leaving it adrift below the cliffs.

Due to the delay in reaching Pointe-du-Hoc, Rudder changed the landing plans and signaled all nine surviving LCAs and three DUKWs to head directly for the east side of Pointe-du-Hoc, with Co D landing between Cos E and F instead of on the more distant western side. At 0709hrs, almost 40 minutes behind schedule, the radio signal "Crowbar" was sent from ML 304 to the rest of the fleet, indicating that the flotillas had touched down. This message was widely received. The unanticipated delay meant that the German defenders had about 45 minutes to recover from the final naval bombardment. ML 304 noticed German soldiers beginning to emerge along the cliff over the landing area, and so unleashed about 20 rounds of 3-pdr and a thousand rounds of 20mm Oerlikon automatic cannon against them. At 0715hrs, Cmdr J. W. Marshall directed his destroyer USS *Satterlee* to close on Pointe-du-Hoc and provide close fire support against German troops appearing along the cliff-tops using its 5in

This photo was taken some days after the landings and shows the gouge in the cliff below the east Flak bunker, with extension ladder, toggle ropes, and rope ladders in place. (NARA)

31

COUNTERATTACK AND RELIEF OF POINTE-DU-HOC, JUNE 6–7, 1944

The area detailed on this map is 2642m wide and 2170m deep.

AU GUAY

CHATEAU DE MR. LE BARON

US FORCES
Ranger Force A   **1** – **17**

1 Force A defense line (Capt. Masny)

2 Co. F, 2nd Rangers

3 Force A headquarters, medics station

4 Advance force, Co. D

5 Advance Force, Co. E

6 Advance Force, Co. F

7 Advance force, 5th Rangers

8 Advance Force command post

9 Advance force outpost (Sgt. Petty) for the
   perimeter of June 6–7

**Relief Force, 116th Regimental Combat Team
(Lt. Col. John Metcalfe, June 7)**

10 Co. B, 743rd Tank Battalion (June 7)

11 Composite company, 2nd Rangers (Forces B/C,
   June 7)

12 Cos. C, D, 5th Rangers

**Relief Force, 116th Regimental Combat Team
(Col. Charles Canham, June 8)**

13 1/116th Infantry (June 8)

14 3/116th Infantry (June 8)

15 2/116th Infantry (reserve force, June 8)

16 Cos. A, B, 743rd Tank Battalion (June 8)

17 Co. B, 743rd Tank Battalion (reserve force, June 8)

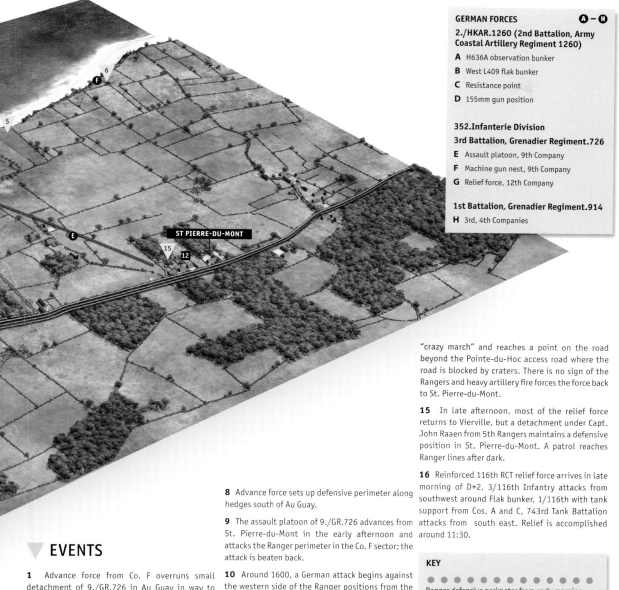

ST PIERRE-DU-MONT

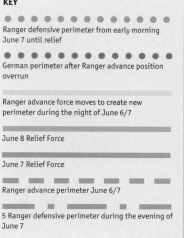

"crazy march" and reaches a point on the road beyond the Pointe-du-Hoc access road where the road is blocked by craters. There is no sign of the Rangers and heavy artillery fire forces the force back to St. Pierre-du-Mont.

15 In late afternoon, most of the relief force returns to Vierville, but a detachment under Capt. John Raaen from 5th Rangers maintains a defensive position in St. Pierre-du-Mont. A patrol reaches Ranger lines after dark.

16 Reinforced 116th RCT relief force arrives in late morning of D+2. 3/116th Infantry attacks from southwest around Flak bunker, 1/116th with tank support from Cos. A and C, 743rd Tank Battalion attacks from south east. Relief is accomplished around 11:30.

▼ EVENTS

1 Advance force from Co. F overruns small detachment of 9./GR.726 in Au Guay in way to rendezvous.

2 Advance force from Cos. D and E meet at assembly point and head to Grandcamp road.

3 Patrol from Co. D finds German guns, spikes two.

4 Patrol from Co. E finds guns, spikes all 5, destroys propellant store.

5 Machine gun nest on cliff to east of Pointe-du-Hoc harasses command bunker until shelled by destroyer in late morning.

6 Machine gun nest of 9./GR.726 harasses Rangers on Pointe-du-Hoc for most of morning until shelled by destroyers.

7 Patrol under Capt. Masny attempts to attack western Flak bunker but thrown back by small arms and artillery fire.

8 Advance force sets up defensive perimeter along hedges south of Au Guay.

9 The assault platoon of 9./GR.726 advances from St. Pierre-du-Mont in the early afternoon and attacks the Ranger perimeter in the Co. F sector; the attack is beaten back.

10 Around 1600, a German attack begins against the western side of the Ranger positions from the remaining German positions on Pointe-du-Hoc. The attack is beaten back by mortar fire.

11 The first of the night attacks by 3./GR.914 begin against the advance party along the hedge. The first attack dissolves after an artillery propellant cache is detonated.

12 The second attack by 3./GR.914 penetrates Ranger defenses around "The Angle" and without a reserve, the Rangers are unable to counter-attack.

13 The third and final attack by 3./GR.914 overwhelms the Co. E positions around 0300. The Germans take about 20 prisoners, and the surviving Rangers except for isolated Co. D retreat back to Pointe-du-Hoc in the darkness.

14 A relief column from the 116th Regimental Combat Team advanced up the Grandcamp on its guns and 40mm anti-aircraft guns. The naval fire support "kept the Germans from being too obnoxious," according to one US Navy account.

The nine LCAs landed along a narrow beach about 30 yards deep and 500 yards wide. The insertion of Co D into the landing area pushed Co F far to the southeast, and outside the strongpoint's perimeter. For many of the seasick and water-soaked Rangers, the landing on firm ground was a welcome relief after hours in rough seas. The heavy bombardment had left numerous deep craters all along the beach, which posed a significant problem as the troops started to disembark. Some troops fell into unseen craters hidden by the surf, while the troops on one LCA were forced to wade through a deep crater when the craft grounded on its lip. With all nine LCAs firmly ashore, the cliffs loomed directly overhead.

Attempts to scale the cliffs with the J-Projectors on the LCA had mixed results. The long trip to the beach and the heavy swell had soaked most of the ropes and made them much heavier than usual. As a result, when the rockets were fired, the grapnels often failed to reach the top of the cliffs. Of the 54 J-projectors on the LCAs, only 19 grapnels were successfully launched over the cliff edge. The LCA 887 team fired two J-projectors on reaching the beach, but recognizing the problem posed by the waterlogged ropes, dismantled the remaining four launchers and carried them to shore. Sgt John Cripps then launched the rockets by hand using a battery, becoming injured and partly blinded by the launch blast. Only two of the smaller Schmuerly rockets were successfully fired, both with the LCA 861 team. Although the bomb craters had interfered with a smooth disembarkation from the craft, the bombardment had caused the collapse of sections of the cliff, leaving high heaps of spoil below the huge gouges in the cliff face. The cliffs were biocalcarenite formed from the compression of ancient seashells in a clay-like matrix. The massive gouges in the cliff provided an opportunity to use the metal ladders, and the teams from both LCA 888 and LCA 668 were able to surmount the cliff using these. Climbing the ropes proved to be a major challenge even in the areas with little German resistance, as their water-logged state and contact with the cliff face made them muddy and very slippery.

The craters and the beach shingle made it impossible to use the Ladder-DUKWs, which could not get close enough to the cliff to deploy the ladders properly. The

Here is the view from the slit at the front of the command bunker that was attacked by teams from Co E. The bunker looks very different today, as the thin appliqué of cement and stone used to camouflage the rounded ferro-concrete casting has been chipped off over the years.

DUKW commanded by Sgt William Stivison decided to try anyway, erecting its ladder to permit the use of the two Lewis guns at the top to provide fire support. Stivison clutched firmly to the top of the ladder 80ft off the ground, and swung dangerously from side to side due to the lack of firm footing for either the DUKW or the ladder, spraying the cliff tops erratically with machine-gun fire. In spite of Stivison's valiant and short-lived effort, the Ladder-DUKWs proved useless.

German resistance to the landings was light due to the casualties inflicted by the bombardment and the naval gunfire, plus the displacement of many of the gun crews outside the perimeter to the south. With the motor launch and destroyer *Satterlee* firing on any sign of movement, some of the German troops remained in craters or trenches and lobbed hand-grenades over the cliff edge. After a while, many Rangers grew contemptuous of the grenades, as they were usually thrown blindly and exploded too far away to do much harm. At least one of the roller-mines was detonated over the heads of the LCA 861 team, temporarily burying one soldier from the ensuing cave-in, but otherwise not injuring any of the team.

The two main centers of German resistance were the observation bunker at the tip of the point and a cluster of soldiers from the Werfer-Regiment 84 section on the cliff edge south of the Flak bunker, armed with a few MG42 machine-guns. Heavy machine-gun fire on the left flank made it impossible for the LCA 884 team to use the four ropes they had launched over the cliff, and they were forced to use the ropes of the neighboring LCA 883. By the time that the first wave of Rangers reached the top of the cliffs, casualties on the shore below amounted to about 15 wounded, mainly from machine-gun fire.

At first, the fighting on the cliff-top was sporadic and light. On the right flank, the Co E team from LCAs 861, 862, and 888 went over the cliff edge and headed for their objective without seeing any Germans on the top. In the center, the first two Rangers from the Co E team from LCA 722 spotted a small group of German troops throwing grenades over the cliff to their right; they hit three with BAR fire, and the rest retreated to the neighboring bunkers. The first Ranger from the Co D team from LCA 668 was killed by German fire on reaching the cliff-top, but the rest of the team was able to surmount the cliff and head off on their assignments without encountering any Germans. The other two Co D teams from LCA 887 and 858 also encountered no Germans on reaching the cliff top, though there was plenty of scattered rifle and machine-gun fire. The team from Co E on LCA 884 was the only one to face serious opposition, and the four ropes they launched over the cliff edge remained unusable, as the cliff top remained under continual fire from nearby Werfer-Regiment 84 machine-gunners. As a result, they joined the neighboring LCA 883 teams and were able to get up the cliffs without much further opposition. The landscape on top of the cliffs was so churned up by bomb craters and heaps of earth and debris that the fields of fire were very short. One soldier from the Werfer-Regiment 84 machine-gun section later recalled that he never saw a single American soldier on top of the Pointe-du-Hoc that entire morning, even though teams from Co F passed by within only a few dozen yards of his trench.

The Ranger advance on the German gun pits provides a text-book example of why the Rangers were chosen for this assignment and not ordinary infantry. Without centralized direction, the individual Ranger teams headed off on their assignments as soon as they had climbed the cliff. No one was shouting orders or prodding reluctant soldiers to move forward. The Rangers swarmed over Pointe-du-Hoc in nine separate little groups, all with a central purpose in mind – to locate and destroy the guns. The extent of the devastation surprised most of the Rangers. While they had expected some bomb damage, it was hard to imagine the total obliteration of nearly all

OVERLEAF
The arrival of the 2nd Rangers at the foot of the cliffs on the western side of Pointe-du-Hoc led to immediate attempts to surmount the cliffs before the German defenders could recover from the preliminary air-attacks and naval gunfire. The plans hinged on the use of rocket-propelled ropes with grapnels fired from the decks of the LCA to assist the climb, as can be seen on the right side of the illustration. However, the long run into the beach left the ropes water-logged, and many ropes failed to make purchase on the cliff tops. The Rangers had alternatives, including the use of multi-section ladders as seen on the left side of the illustration. In addition, the LCA brought along smaller, hand-emplaced rocket launchers for propelling lighter ropes with grapnels up the cliff as can be seen with one of the Rangers immediately to the left of the LCA. Although not evident in this view, the collapse of several sections of cliff due to aerial bombardment and naval gunfire significantly accelerated the climb in some sections of the beach. The weakness of the German defenses, the redundant means for overcoming the cliffs, and the dogged determination of the Rangers led to a speedy and successful conclusion to the first stage of the mission. Now it was up to the Rangers to locate and destroy the guns.

The decision to have Co D land with the other two companies on the east cliffs pushed the LCAs delivering Company F southward, beyond the battery perimeter. This photo, taken a few days after the raid, shows the bomb cratering along the beach and the Flak bunker/command post (1). The location of the five guns is barely evident in the background of the photo (2).

recognizable landmarks. Aside from the two large gun casemates and the observation bunker, nearly everything else was deleted with massive bomb craters and submerged under heaps of earth and debris. The Rangers were convinced that the Germans were using underground tunnels, as they would pop up unexpectedly all over the site. In fact, few of the covered communication trenches had survived the incessant bombing, but there was an abundance of small bunkers, Tobruks, and other underground shelters that the Pointe-du-Hoc garrison had used as shelter prior to the bombing, many of them invisible under the dirt and debris.

The gun pits were not far from the eastern cliff edge, so Ranger teams quickly reached their objectives. Co E was assigned to overcome the observation bunker and gun pit 3. The observation bunker was the only site on Pointe-du-Hoc that remained in German hands and it would hold out for more than a day. The first two Rangers from the LCA 861 team began approaching the observation bunker from the front and soon came under small-arms fire from the bunker slit. Using the craters in front of the bunker for cover, Sgt Charles Denbo and Pvt Harry Roberts got within grenade range and managed to throw three or four grenades through the slit. Denbo was wounded by rifle fire, but four more Rangers under Lt Theodore Lapres soon joined them in front of the bunker, including Sgt Andrew Yardley with a bazooka. One bazooka rocket detonated against the edge of the firing slit, but the second passed through the slit and exploded inside.

With Yardley providing cover, the rest of the Rangers moved to the rear of the bunker. While the LCA 861 team had been moving on the bunker from the front, five Rangers under Lt Joseph Leagans from the neighboring LCA 862 had been advancing near the bunker towards their objective, gun pit 3, when they saw a German throwing grenades over the cliff from a trench near the bunker. They threw grenades at the enemy soldier, which forced him to retreat into the observation bunker. On reaching the rear of the bunker, they could hear a radio in use and so shot off the antenna. A grenade was tossed into the entrance foyer below, but the steel door was proof against any infantry weapons. Leagans decided to move on to their objective, leaving Cpl Victor Aguzzi to guard the rear entrance of the bunker until a demolition team could be sent. Moments afterwards, Yardley's team joined up with Aguzzi, with neither team having been aware of each other's actions in the vicinity of the bunker. Since they did not have demolition charges, Yardley ordered two soldiers to remain in a trench in front of the bunker, keeping it under watch while Cpl Aguzzi kept the back entrance covered. A final assault on the observation bunker was not made until D+1. In a separate action nearby, the Co E commander, Capt Gilbert Baugh, was seriously wounded while leading an attack on a German position housed in one of the bunkers. Most of the personnel bunkers had associated Tobruk machine-gun pits, and these were a frequent source of trouble for the advancing Rangers.

While the fighting took place around the observation bunker, teams from Co D were converging on gun pits 4, 5, and 6 on the western side of site. On reaching the remains of the gun pits, the Rangers quickly determined that the guns were not present. The gun pits were filled with the earth and the shattered remains of the camouflage netting, and fake timber guns. This side of Pointe-du-Hoc promontory was the most dangerous, as the 37mm Flak cannon on the western Flak bunker had not been knocked out due to its remoteness from the rest of the site. There was a clear line of fire from the Flak bunker toward the three western gun pits, and any Rangers venturing too near the western side of the site were brought under 37mm cannon fire as well as machine-gun and rifle fire. It is not clear from available accounts if the 88mm gun there was still functional after the air raids. The western Flak bunker would remain the main source of German resistance within the strongpoint for the next two days; at least one account suggests that the battery commander used it as his command post during the fighting. When Co F reached gun pits 1 and 2 on the eastern side, they found the pits abandoned as well.

The original plan had been for the Rangers to move through the battery after eliminating the guns, and take control of the Vierville–Grandcamp road further south outside the battery position. Three teams set off for the road, from Co D (LCA 858), Co E (LCA 888), and Co F (LCA 887). The teams from Co D and Co E gradually converged on the ruins of the Guelinel farm, encountering a substantial amount of small-arms fire and occasional German artillery and mortar fire, as well as a few German patrols. The farm was near the edge of the strongpoint, and the main defensive orientation had been along this perimeter, which accounted for the greater density of German resistance points. The fighting was not well organized on either side and the cratered landscape made it difficult to see any significant distance. In some cases Ranger patrols passed within earshot of German patrols, with neither side actually encountering the other. The Rangers were pushed along by a creeping barrage behind them, a pre-planned naval bombardment that was proving to be a hazard and that could not be stopped due to a lack of radio communication between the forward Ranger teams and either the Ranger headquarters or the ships. After suffering about a dozen casualties in encounters with the German defenders, the teams from Cos D and E reached the Grandcamp road around 0815hrs. The amount of German small-arms fire lightened, as by this time the Rangers were outside the strongpoint.

As Co F had landed so much further south than planned, the Co F team under Lt Robert Arman was on the cliffs outside the strongpoint and so moved through the anti-glider barriers and minefield on its southeastern side, and finally to the Grandcamp road, reaching it around 0805hrs. They began advancing along the road to the west when they were brought under fire from a German resistance nest in the hamlet of Au Guay. The Germans were not especially determined, and some BAR fire convinced them to surrender. The three Ranger teams met on the Grandcamp road shortly afterwards, with the Ranger advance detachment at this point numbering about 50 troops. At this point, the mission was to secure the road and defend the Ranger positions in the Pointe-du-Hoc battery from German attacks, most likely to emanate

**JUNE 6
1944**

**0709hrs:
Ranger Force A
lands at
Pointe-du-Hoc**

from the south and west. The Rangers were not as concerned about a German advance from the east and instead were expecting that a force of Rangers and the 116th RCT would arrive momentarily from Omaha Beach. After establishing defensive outposts along the road, both Co D and Co E sent out small patrols to reconnoiter.

Sgt Leonard Lomell and Sgt Jack Kuhn from Co D moved forward of their outpost and decided to use a path running south between two parallel hedgerows to avoid the intermittent sniper fire. About 250 yards from the road were the five surviving German guns, in battery position and pointing to the west toward the Vire estuary and Utah Beach. The guns were unguarded and unmanned, but the battery positions included ammunition and were ready for action. Lomell had two thermite grenades, which he jammed into the traverse mechanisms of the two guns to disable them, and then smashed the gun sights on a third gun. The team returned to the Co D outpost to get more grenades. In the meantime, a Co E patrol of five Rangers under Sgt Frank Rupinski had been advancing towards the hedgerow from the east and located the guns shortly after Lomell and Kuhn's departure. They had enough thermite grenades to place one in each gun tube and spike all the guns, and they also removed the gun sights and threw them away. Before departing, they blew up the main cache of propellant charges. As Rupinski's men were at work on the guns, Lomell and a reinforced team from Co D returned to the gun position, but on seeing the Co E Rangers at work, headed back to their outpost. Two Co D runners were sent back to Pointe-du-Hoc by separate routes to inform Rudder that the guns had been spiked; Co E sent its own runners. Rudder's HQ sent messages by radio, signal lamp, and pigeon at 1110hrs to higher headquarters. Neither the V Corps headquarters nor any other Army unit ever received the radio message, though it would appear that one pigeon reached England safely.

Securing Pointe-du-Hoc

While several teams and patrols were establishing the outer defenses of Pointe-du-Hoc, the majority of the Rangers were attempting to secure Pointe-du-Hoc itself and to establish communication with higher headquarters. Although there was no organized resistance in the central part of Pointe-du-Hoc except for the observation bunker, there were several significant resistance points on the periphery of the strongpoint, most notably the western Flak bunker, and a machine-gun position on

A group of Rangers in one of the craters defending Rudder's command post. The Ranger in the center is wearing the assault vest commonly seen on US troops of the first wave on D-Day.

JAMES EARL RUDDER

James Earl Rudder was born on May 6, 1910, in Texas. He attended Tarleton Agricultural College in 1928–29 before completing his degree in industrial education at Texas A&M in 1932; he was a member of the Corps of Cadets and was commissioned a second lieutenant in the US Army Reserves on graduation. He was first employed as a teacher and football coach at Brady High School until 1938, when he moved on to similar positions at Tarleton. He married in 1937 and his family eventually included five children. Like most Army reservists, he was called to active duty in 1941. Rudder attended Infantry School at Ft Benning in the autumn of 1941 and was assigned as a battalion executive officer with the 83rd Division in Indiana. His talents led to his dispatch to the Army's Command and General Staff School at Ft Leavenworth for the fall–winter class of 1942–43, after which he returned to the 83rd Division as assistant division G-3 (operations). The newly formed 2nd Ranger Battalion was originally led by its 41-year-old founder, LtCol William Saffarans, followed by a string of acting battalion commanders. Maj "Big Jim" Rudder was finally assigned to command the battalion and arrived on June 30, 1943. Rudder's vigor, intellect, and leadership skills made him well suited to the demanding task, and he was a lieutenant colonel by the time of the D-Day operation.

Rudder was decorated with the Distinguished Service Cross and Purple Heart for his actions at Pointe-du-Hoc. The 2nd Rangers recuperated from their heavy losses and were sent back into action in August 1944 during the Brittany campaign, including the savage fighting for Brest in September. After another period of recuperation, the battalion was committed to the fighting in the Hürtgen forest in November 1944. Rudder was unhappy that his unit was assigned a minor but costly defensive role, and in early December the 2nd Rangers were assigned to take Hill 400, "Castle Hill," during the final push. Nearly half the 2nd Rangers were casualties after their capture and defense of the hill. While the 2nd Rangers were pulled off the line for yet another reconstruction, Rudder was promoted and assigned to command the 109th Infantry Regiment. This regiment was part of the 28th Division that had been decimated in the Hürtgen forest fighting and had been sent in December 1944 to a "quiet" section of the front in Belgium for rebuilding; the division was commanded by another D-Day hero, MajGen Norman Cota, who had uttered the legendary "Rangers, lead the way!" command on Dog White beach. The 28th

James Earl Rudder © (NARA)

Division was directly in the path of the German Ardennes offensive and fought a desperate rearguard action on the approaches to Bastogne. Rudder's distinguished service during the 1944–45 campaigns led to numerous decorations, including the Silver Star and Bronze Star with Oak Leaf Cluster.

Rudder was released from active duty in April 1946 with the rank of colonel and went back to civilian life in Texas; he remained active in the Army reserve, becoming a brigadier general in 1954 and major general in 1957, taking command of the 90th (Reserve) Infantry Division in 1957 and finally retiring from Army service in 1967. He was mayor of Brady, Texas, from 1946 to 1952 and later went into business. In 1955 he was appointed Commissioner of the General Land Office, a state position of considerable importance due to its role in oil leases, and a post previously embroiled in scandal. Rudder's reforms led to his election to the position in 1956 and he served through 1958. An ancillary aspect of his role as land commissioner was in replenishing the state's university funds, and his personal attention to this responsibility led to his appointment as vice president of his alma mater, Texas A&M. He became the college president in 1959 and led the transformation of Texas A&M from a small land-grant college to one of America's premier university systems. He was awarded the Distinguished Service Medal by fellow Texan President Lyndon Johnson in 1967, the highest peacetime service award. Rudder died in 1970 at age 59.

the cliffs about 1,500 yards to the east outside the strongpoint. There were also a number of German soldiers in bunkers and trenches within the strongpoint, some of them still tunneling out after the entrances were buried in the pre-dawn bombing. Ranger casualties in the most daunting phase of the operation, the assault on the cliffs, had proven to be much lighter than expected. However, casualties were rapidly mounting in the numerous small skirmishes occurring both within and outside the Pointe-du-Hoc strongpoint.

LtCol Rudder assigned Capt Otto Masny, commander of Co F, the task of securing Pointe-du-Hoc. Masny attempted to clear out the western Flak bunker with a squad of Rangers, but ran into a storm of fire and was forced to retire. Through the course of the day, about 40 German prisoners were taken during the mop-up operations and by the advance group on the Grandcamp road.

Rudder established the Ranger HQ next to the eastern Flak bunker. The bombing had dislodged a large chunk of the cliff near the bunker, and LCA 668 had placed a ladder on top of the rocky debris, providing good access to the crater near the bunker. The HQ communications officer, Lt James Eikner, had begun transmitting messages by the battalion HQ SCR-284 radio from the base of the cliff, and when Rudder established his command post, Eikner followed. Radio communication within Ranger Force A proved difficult in part on account of widespread failure of equipment due to immersion in sea water during the wet ride to shore. The platoons each had a SCR-536 "Handie-Talkie" AM radio, while each company HQ, including Rudder's HQ company, had a SCR-300 "Walkie-Talkie" FM radio with an effective range of about 3 miles; unfortunately few were functioning. In addition, the NSFCP under Lt Kenneth Norton and the Army 293rd Assault Signal Company forward observer party under Capt Jonathan Harwood had their own radios, but these were water-logged and inoperable. Pvt Henry Genther attempted to repair one of the fire control radios in one of the German gun casemates, and once he got it working Rudder, along with Norton and Harwood, went to the bunker in mid-morning to communicate with USS *Texas*.

Rudder set up his HQ in the eastern Flak bunker, immediately above one of the sections of the cliff that had collapsed under naval gun fire. This is a view of the eastern side of the bunker on D+2 after the arrival of the relief column, with German prisoners being marched away in the background.

The first reinforcements for Rudder's Rangers arrived on the afternoon of D+1 aboard LCVPs like this one. As can be seen, large craters from Operation *Flashlamp* proved to be a hazard crossing the beach. (NARA)

For reasons that remain unclear, one of the warships, apparently HMS *Glasgow*, brought the casemate under fire. A projectile hit the exterior of the casemate, killing Harwood and Genther and wounding Norton. Rudder was soaked in yellow marker dye from the impact of the projectile and was dazed but not injured. In spite of the concussion and a previous bullet wound in the thigh from earlier in the morning, Rudder remained in active command through the operation. Rudder's valiant leadership has been widely praised by the surviving Rangers. Lt Dutch Vermeer later wrote that "I cannot pay a high enough tribute to Col Rudder… Under the leadership of Col Rudder, miracles almost seemed possible." Inspiration also came from the British liaison observer, LtCol Thomas Trevor, a combat-hardened Commando. Even though wounded by a bullet through his helmet during the landing, Trevor's calm demeanor provided welcome reassurance for the well-trained but inexperienced Rangers.

Initial communication between the Rangers and the Navy was hampered by radio problems, but Eikner had shown the foresight to purchase an EE-84 signal lamp in England. This was used to establish initial communications with the *Satterlee* at 0728hrs, though eventually radio communications were established. The communications link between the cliff-top command post and the US Navy and Royal Navy destroyers was absolutely vital for the Rangers, as all efforts to establish communications with Ranger Forces B and C failed, as did attempts to communicate with V Corps and the 116th RCT. The first radio contact between Force A and the 116th Infantry Regiment on Omaha Beach did not take place until 0615hrs on D+1, and was sporadic and inconclusive at best. Communication with the advance force on the Grandcamp road was also difficult, though eventually field telephone wires were connected between Rudder's command post and the dispersed companies along the road.

The Navy proved to be the Rangers' main lifeline to the outside world. In the afternoon, the Rangers requested that the Navy send a craft to shore to help extract the many wounded. A boat arrived from the destroyer USS *Barton* around 1430hrs, but German machine-gun fire from the cliffs east of Pointe-du-Hoc wounded the boat crew and prevented the vessel from landing.

The Artillery Threat

German mortar and artillery fire intensified during the day as Pointe-du-Hoc was brought under fire from the two artillery batteries to the southwest near Maisy. These were elements of the 716.Infanterie-Division's artillery regiment and were part of the Vire River strongpoint group (*Stützpunkt Gruppe Vire*). This artillery concentration is worth exploring in a bit more detail, as in recent years it has become the center of

The naval gunfire led to the collapse of several areas of the Pointe-du-Hoc cliff, including this one immediately below the east Flak bunker. The spoil below the collapse made it easier for the Rangers to erect ladders, and this particular site became the main access and debarkation point for the Rangers on D+1 and D+2. (NARA)

JUNE 6 1944

1000hrs: German HQ realizes that the assault on Pointe-du-Hoc is not a small-scale raid

a controversy relating to the Pointe-du-Hoc raid. The 8th battery of Artillerie-Regiment 1716 (8./AR.1716) in WN 84 was codenamed "Brasilia" and located near Maisy-la-Martinière; it was armed with four Skoda 100mm Model 14/19 light field howitzers. This site was being fortified with the construction of H669 casemates in June 1944, with two near completion, so the four howitzers were in open field positions nearby, the main site being called T16 (Target 16) on the Allied bombardment charts and the field deployment as T16A. The neighboring 9./AR.1716 was in WN 83 near Maisy-la-Perruque and was armed with four 155mm Schneider Model 1917 howitzers in kettle gun pits; Allied intelligence called it T5. The batteries had five forward observation posts along the coast stretching between resistance nests WN 79 and WN 92, the easternmost located on the western outskirts of Grandcamp and the westernmost outside Géfosse. They had pre-registered targets along this same stretch of coastline on the eastern side of the Vire River estuary, as well as a number of targets on the opposite bank. The two batteries were almost equidistant between Utah and Omaha Beaches. According to surviving German artillery maps, the 9./AR.1716 battery could barely reach the western side of the Vierville draw on Omaha Beach; however, both batteries could reach Utah Beach, even though it was in another division's sector.

Both batteries had been engaged by pre-D-Day air attacks, but not on the scale of prime targets such as Pointe-du-Hoc or Longues-sur-Mer. Neither was a primary target of the preliminary naval bombardment plan, but one or both batteries began firing towards Utah Beach after dawn, drawing the wrath of warships from the Utah Beach bombardment group. The USS *Herndon* was the first to engage the batteries around 0655hrs, and twice more through 0815hrs. Around 0740hrs, the destroyer USS *Shubrick* was provided coordinates of the batteries from a spotter plane and engaged them with 5in fire. Although this temporarily halted the German gunfire, at 0820hrs the Maisy batteries tried to engage *Shubrick* with data from their forward observer bunkers on the coast. The *Shubrick* responded, and again temporarily silenced the bunkers. Around noon, the Maisy batteries again tried to strike targets on Utah Beach and this time were targeted by the cruiser HMS *Hawkins* and the

Dutch gunboat HNMS *Soemba*. After these engagements, the Maisy batteries turned their attention on Pointe-du-Hoc based on requests from GR.726, but the *Soemba* remained on call and continued to fire on the batteries based on requests from NSFCP-1 at Pointe-du-Hoc.

Although the Maisy batteries continued to harass the Rangers at Pointe-du-Hoc for the next two days, the recent controversy has little to do with the actual fighting. There have been sensational claims that the battery played a crucial role in bombarding Omaha Beach, that the Pointe-du-Hoc battery was in fact a clever German ruse, and the Maisy batteries the real artillery threat. However, the evidence suggests that the Maisy batteries played a more mundane role in the D-Day battles, as they were outside the range of Omaha Beach and were used in their assigned mission towards the Vire estuary and later in support of the GR.726 and GR.914 counterattacks against nearby Pointe-du-Hoc.

**JUNE 6
1944**

**1600hrs:
German
counterattack
begins**

Ranger Force B: In the Devil's Garden

Ranger Force B commanded by Capt Ralph Goranson consisted of 68 Rangers of C/2nd Rangers, and was carried to Normandy aboard the LSI(S)-1 *Prince Charles* along with the associated 501st LCA Flotilla. The plan was to land on Omaha Beach Charlie at H+3 alongside A/116th Infantry Regiment, and to proceed westward over the cliffs, clear out the German positions at Pointe-et-Raz-de-la-Percée that threatened the right flank of the 116th Infantry landing, and then to proceed to Pointe-du-Hoc, destroying any German installations along the route taken. C/116th Infantry was to provide flanking protection and a platoon of Duplex Drive (DD) amphibious tanks from the 743rd Tank Battalion were to be "on call" for support.

The plans for landing on Dog Green sector seriously underestimated the German defenses in *Stützpunkt Vierville*, undoubtedly the most formidable fortified area of the Normandy beaches. The strongpoint included two resistance nests, WN 71 and WN 72, covering each side of the Vierville draw, a ravine that led from the coast back to the town of Vierville-sur-Mer, and a series of beach obstructions that the Germans had dubbed "the Devil's Garden." The Vierville strongpoint was covered by enfilade fire from resistance nests WN 73 and WN 74 in the cliffs to the west of Dog Green that extended to Pointe-et-Raz-de-la-Percée. This sector was held by 9./GR.726 in the

Here is a view of the Vierville draw taken shortly after the war. Some of the German fortifications of WN 72 (1) still remain, blocking the entrance to the Vierville draw. The area where Force B climbed the cliffs is shown as well as the fortified house (2) from WN 73, which was the center of most of the fighting by Goranson's small force. Force C landed further east to the left of the picture. (MHI)

This is the view from a PaK 40 75mm antitank gun position of GR.916 carved in the hillside on the western side of the Vierville draw and overlooking Dog Charlie Beach. (NARA)

bunkers, reinforced by elements of GR.916 in field emplacements. The kill-zone in front of *Stützpunkt Vierville* had already been pre-registered by 2./AR.352 as well as by mortars in the strongpoints.

LCA 418 with Lt Bill Moody's 1st Platoon and LCA 1038 with Lt Sid Salomon's 2nd Platoon left the *Prince Charles* at 0427hrs, about an hour before dawn. Unlike Rudder's three companies at Pointe-du-Hoc, who were traveling light due to the cliffs, the Rangers of Co C were heavily burdened with enough supplies for five days. The craft began making for shore behind the LCTs carrying the 743rd Tank Battalion and the LCAs carrying Co A, 116th Infantry.

As the first waves of landing craft arrived in front of the Vierville strongpoint, they were raked with mortar and machine-gun fire that increased in intensity once the bow ramps were dropped. A/116th Infantry suffered horrendous casualties, with one LCA taking a direct artillery hit in the front, and another was shattered by mortar fire. More casualties were suffered as the first wave of LCAs landed in front of *Stützpunkt Vierville* at 0636hrs. The two Ranger LCAs arrived nine minutes after A/116th Infantry, on the western side of *Stützpunkt Vierville* at 0645hrs. Lt Moody led the 1st Platoon off LCA 418, but the craft had its bow-ramp blown away and received two other strike by mortars or gunfire. Many of the Rangers, including Capt Goranson in the rear of the craft, exited over the side to avoid the heavy fire directed against the bow. Lt Salomon led the 2nd Platoon off LCA 1038, but the second Ranger at the ramp was hit immediately by machine-gun fire and a mortar round struck inside the personnel hold. The surviving Rangers, seasick, slowed down by excessive gear, and under continual machine-gun and mortar fire, had to cross more than 300 yards of surf and beach for the relative safety of the cliff. From the time the ramps went down to the time the Rangers reached the cliff, they suffered 54 percent casualties: 19 killed, 13 seriously wounded, and 5 lightly wounded. Capt Goranson was hit nine times but, miraculously, the bullets only hit his gear and he was not wounded.

The shell-shocked A/116th Infantry had lost all its officers and most of its NCOs; its infantrymen huddled behind German beach obstructions, where they continued to be picked off by German riflemen and machine-guns. Following their training, the Rangers rapidly moved off the beach, trying to encourage the infantrymen to follow. Salomon and the survivors of the 2nd Platoon immediately set about climbing the cliff in front of them, but by the time they had reached the top, only nine of the platoon's original 32 men were left. The 1st Platoon and Capt Goranson soon followed by finding a section where free-hand climbing was possible, and then lowering ropes. Goranson led an attack to clear a stone house that was part of the WN 73 defenses. The Rangers then began to clear the trenches, mortar pits, and machine-gun nests in the vicinity. They were eventually joined by about 20 infantrymen from B/116th Infantry, who used the 1st Platoon ropes. Force B was obliged to remain in the midst of WN 73 though the early afternoon due to the continual arrival of more German troops from Vierville; the Rangers claimed that some 69 Germans troops were killed and Force B suffered two more casualties while on top the cliff. As the fighting subsided, Goranson led a patrol to Pointe-et-Raz-de-la-Percée around 1430hrs, but as they were approaching the site it was blasted by US Navy destroyers. In the late afternoon, after contact was made with the 116th Infantry, the survivors of Force B moved down from to the Vierville ravine, and then joined up with Ranger Force C.

Ranger Force C: Pointe-du-Hoc or Vierville?

The third and final element of the Ranger Group to land was Force C consisting of the remaining two companies of the 2nd Rangers and all of the 5th Rangers. Force C was commanded by LtCol Max Schneider of the 5th Rangers. The naval component of Force C consisted of three LCA flotillas, led to shore by ML 163. After forming up, they left the Transport Area at 0540hrs and reached the start line off Dog Green at 0708hrs, where ML 163 instructed the LCA to stop engines and await orders. The codeword "Crowbar" had been received, indicating that Rudder's force A had landed at Pointe-du-Hoc, and the Rangers eagerly awaited the signal that would indicate that Rudder's forces had successfully surmounted the cliffs. Had this radio signal been received, Force C would have altered course and set out to Pointe-du-Hoc to reinforce Rudder. The Rangers set up one of their SCR-284 radios in an LCA and tried to reach Rudder and the command ship *Prince Charles*, but failed to make contact. Cdr Dennis on *Prince Charles*, having failed to receive the signal and not seeing the alternate flare signals from Pointe-du-Hoc, decided to follow the plan and order the three flotillas to land on Dog Green. However, the radio on ML 163 also failed but the Fairmile led the flotillas towards Dog Green according to plan.

The 501st Flotilla containing Cos A and B, 2nd Rangers, was on the right side of the assault wave and heading towards the eastern shoulder of the Vierville draw into the *Stützpunkt Vierville* kill-zone. At 200 yards from the first line of Element C beach obstructions, the flotilla came under concentrated mortar fire. One of the Co A LCA lost 20 of 34 men to machine-gun fire before reaching the seawall; the other craft did little better. All the Co A officers were killed or wounded on the beach. The unit after-action report grimly noted that "By 0805, all the men surviving the beach holocaust were reorganizing under cover of the fortified-house line." The remnants of Co A under their NCOs stormed the WN 70 machine-gun nest, which had been responsible for many of their casualties, on the bluff in front of them.

LCA 401 carrying the 2nd Platoon of Co B had its bow blown off; the platoon leader and several men were severely wounded and the craft gradually sank. As the remaining vessels began maneuvering through the obstacles a few moments later, machine-gun fire also began to strike the craft; the LCAs touched down at 0752hrs. LCA 458 was so badly hit that it remained drifting amongst the obstacles. One of the Royal Navy officers aboard LCA 421 later reported that "the water between the beach and C Element was full of soldiers apparently from the initial waves, trying to get what cover they could from the sweeping machine-gun fire, by lying prone in the sea or kneeling behind obstructions." The Rangers followed their training and attempted to race across the hundred yards of beach. Of the 68 Co B troops, only 2 officers and 25 men reached the seawall. The 1st Platoon, Co B, under Capt Edgar Arnold, attempted to clear WN 71 in the east side of the Vierville draw in cooperation with a platoon of DD tanks from the 743rd Tank Battalion. This platoon was not enough to accomplish this mission, and eventually returned to the beach, and followed the rest of the unit over the bluffs. (This action has been immortalized in the opening scenes of the film *Saving*

A view of *Stützpunkt Vierville* taken from the USS *Texas* on D-Day, with smoke rising from the Vierville draw following the bombardment sometime between 1200 and 1300hrs. Goranson's Force B landed in front of the cliffs on the right side of the photo, while Schneider's 5th Rangers landed in front of the bluff on the left side of the photo. The Vierville church was hit by the destroyer USS *Harding* around 1400hrs, due to concerns that it was being used as an observation post by German artillery. (NARA)

Private Ryan.) The 2nd Platoon, Co B, headed directly over the bluff following Co A, and was the first to join up with the neighboring 5th Rangers. They offered to lead a patrol to Pointe-du-Hoc, but this was vetoed by LtCol Schneider due to the horrific casualties suffered by the unit.

The 504th Flotilla under the command of Lt J. McA. F. Cassidy, RNVR, was supposed to land its complement from the 5th Rangers immediately after the beleaguered 501st Flotilla. Seeing the carnage ashore, and realizing that the numerous damaged craft and obstacles would hinder a landing, Lt Cassidy decided to land his craft further to the left due to the presence of several DD tanks and some smoke cover. He later recounted that "For the last 30 yards, the beaching of each craft became an individual effort by coxswains who had to weave their craft through well-placed obstructions with Teller mines fixed to the top; this was made all the more difficult by a swell and following sea. All coxswains reported that the Rangers landed without any casualties and only had to wade ashore in water up to their knees." The same situation was repeated on the 507th Flotilla, with LtCol Schneider and the Royal Navy ensigns deciding to head for a clear landing spot to the left of the 504th Flotilla. This change of plans had a dramatic effect on the fate of the 5th Rangers, and the entire unit landed with very modest casualties. The Rangers advanced over the promenade, a beach road at the base of the bluffs, but were temporarily stopped by a double-apron barbed wire obstruction. Schneider gave the command "Tallyho," starting the advance over the bluff to the rendezvous point prior to heading on to Pointe-du-Hoc. Four gaps were blown in the wire using Bangalore torpedoes.

While Schneider and Maj Sullivan, the battalion executive officer, were conferring, BrigGen Norman Cota, assistant 29th Division commander, appeared. After brief words, Cota uttered the command that would go down in Ranger lore: "Rangers, lead the way!" The bluffs to the east of the Vierville strongpoint had far fewer defenses and the scrub offered some natural shelter during the climb; this sector of the beach was also obscured by smoke from several grass fires, which further aided the Ranger advance to the top of the bluffs. The smoke was so thick at some points that the Rangers used their gas masks. The 5th Rangers were one of the few units to arrive on this stretch of beach in relatively good order, and their characteristic aggressiveness and determination provided the key impetus to surmount the bluffs aside *Stützpunkt Vierville*. While circumstances prevented them from participating in the Pointe-du-Hoc raid, their arrival on Dog White was a major factor in the eventual success of the landings in this sector.

The 5th Rangers reached the top of the bluffs east of *Stützpunkt Vierville* by 0900hrs alongside surviving elements of C/116th Infantry, and were later joined by the remnants of Cos A and B, 2nd Rangers. Schneider ordered Cos B and C, 5th Rangers, to lead the way to the planned assembly area southwest of Vierville-sur-Mer before heading to Pointe-du-Hoc. During the advance, they ran into elements of GR.916, which was moving forward to counterattack the US landings. The ensuing skirmishes tied down the Ranger advance for more than three hours. Schneider finally decided to avoid the strongest German concentrations and to pass directly through the village of Vierville.

Although most of the 5th Rangers had surmounted the bluffs in a group, Capt Charles Parker, commander of Co A, along with 1st Platoon, Co A, led by Lt Stanley Zelepsky, were isolated from the rest of the battalion. Lacking any communication, they followed the plan and headed off for Pointe-du-Hoc on their own, fighting several skirmishes along the way. The 24 men of the patrol took 40 German prisoners and arrived at the Pointe-du-Hoc perimeter around 2100hrs. They had no idea where the rest of the 5th Rangers were located, but told Rudder's men that they thought they were immediately behind.

In fact, the rest of the 5th Rangers, in spite of their best intentions to reach Pointe-du-Hoc, were tied down in the defense of the 116th RCT perimeter around Vierville. The 116th Infantry had suffered higher casualties than any other US regiment on D-Day, due to the bloodbath in front of *Stützpunkt Vierville*, and the Rangers helped fill the gap. The Germans launched counterattacks against the US positions after nightfall, and BrigGen Cota of the 29th Division subordinated the 5th Rangers and the associated elements of the 2nd Rangers to Col Canham's 116th Infantry for the defense of Vierville until the situation was clarified on D+1.

German Counterattack

While the Rangers were attempting to secure Pointe-du-Hoc, the Wehrmacht was planning to counterattack. The 352.Infanterie-Division was informed of the Ranger landing the moment it occurred by the observation bunker; about an hour later at 0815hrs came the ominous news: "no messages from Pointe-du-Hoc." At 0705hrs, 9./GR.726 was ordered to send its platoon in St- Pierre-du-Mont to counterattack what was originally believed to be a weak Commando force. The III./GR.726 consisted of four companies and was subordinated to Oberstleutnant Ernst Goth's

The most persistent source of German resistance within the Pointe-du-Hoc battery site came from the western German Flak bunker on the southwest extremity of the position. This is the view from the Flak bunker toward the main battery position; as can be seen, the 20mm cannon there had a clear field of fire against the Rangers. (MHI)

JUNE 6
1944

2330hrs:
First German
attack against
Ranger advance
detachment on
the Grandcamp
road

GR.916 of 352.Infanterie-Division. In the case of 9./GR.726, this company had been assigned to man the defenses along the cliffs from Pointe-et-Raz-de-la-Percée to Grandcamp; the battalion's other two rifle companies were stationed on the western side of Omaha Beach in the St Laurent and Vierville areas. The 9.Kompanie was thinly spread out in defensive positions along several miles of coastline, and kept an "assault platoon" of about 35 men in St-Pierre-du-Mont as a company reserve, which was the unit given the task of retaking Pointe-du-Hoc. This unit was moving down the Grandcamp–Vierville road around 0830hrs when the Rangers arrived in the area, but at first both sides avoided contact.

By 1000hrs, Goth's HQ realized that the Pointe-du-Hoc attack was not a small-scale Commando raid, but rather a larger raid that was assessed to consist of two companies. The platoon from 9./GR.726 was clearly inadequate for the task, and Goth ordered III./GR.726 to send as many troops as possible to continue the counterattacks against Pointe-du-Hoc. In reality, this force didn't amount to much, as the battalion had only two companies in this sector, the 9th and the 12th (heavy weapons company), both of which were thinly spread out in the coastal defense bunkers from the Vire estuary to Omaha Beach.

The first major German attack of the day took place in the early afternoon, when 9./GR.726 finally advanced from St- Pierre-du-Mont towards the eastern flank of the Ranger positions. This section of the line was held by a force from Co F under Lt Richard Wintz. The Germans set up a MG42 machine-gun to provide covering fire, but the German attack was broken up with rifle fire. An indecisive firefight went on for over an hour before the German platoon withdrew. There was scattered fighting throughout the day, all along the Ranger defensive perimeter, in some cases local efforts by the remnants of the original Pointe-du-Hoc garrison, and in other cases scattered patrols by elements of GR.726. The advance Ranger group on the Grandcamp road captured about 40 German soldiers and killed about 50 during the day's fighting. About 30 of the German casualties were credited to Sgt William Petty, who had established an outpost in an abandoned farm building with a clear field of fire for his BAR. Through the afternoon, the Rangers had suffered a further 44 casualties in Cos E and F, including 10 killed, 24 seriously wounded, and 10 missing.

This is a contemporary photo taken by the author from the western Flak bunker looking eastward towards the main Pointe-du-Hoc battery positions. Here was the center of German resistance on Pointe-du-Hoc for more than two days of fighting.

Casualties were actually higher, as Co D was unable to report its status due to its dispersion, and Rangers who were lightly wounded but still in action were not listed. The defensive position along the perimeter had an effective strength of only 65 men by the late afternoon.

The machine-gun nests from Werfer-Regiment 84 were abandoned in late morning after the regiment ordered its troops to withdraw. This eliminated one source of persistent machine-gun fire along the eastern side of Pointe-du-Hoc. The troublesome machine-gun position further southeast on the cliff east of Pointe-du-Hoc was the subject of a number of attacks. A patrol from Co F attempted to reach the site in the morning, but was frustrated by the distance and German sniping. An airstrike was called in and four P-47 Thunderbolts nearly struck the Ranger command post instead, but the timely display of an American flag prevented that from happening. Finally, in the late afternoon, a destroyer approached the cliff and at point-blank range, obliterated the German position with gunfire.

As 352.Infanterie-Division's GR.916 had its hands full trying to resist the main US landings on Omaha Beach, in the late morning the divisional HQ shifted the regimental boundaries eastward, freeing Goth's GR.916 of responsibility for the Grandcamp sector and Pointe-du-Hoc and turning this sector over to Oberstleutnant Ernst Heyna's GR.914 in the Isigny–Carentan area. Heyna was instructed to deploy two companies of I./GR.914, headquartered at Osmanville, against Pointe-du-Hoc, a distance of about 6.2 miles. However, the battalion had been engaged since the early morning hours in counterattacking scattered US paratroop landings around Isigny, and it took time to collect elements of the battalion's scattered 3rd and 4th companies and move them to the northeast. The I./GR.914 was harassed during movement by Allied air attack and did not arrive in the Pointe-du-Hoc area until the late afternoon. Its mission against Pointe-du-Hoc came under question in the afternoon, when Goth asked the divisional HQ to send the battalion further east to assist GR.916 in continuing counterattacks against the main American landing at Omaha Beach. Oberstleutnant Heyna discouraged this, pointing out that the battalion would have to march to Omaha Beach in daylight hours and would be subjected to decimation by air attack. As a result, its mission against Pointe-du-Hoc was reaffirmed. The presence of Rudder's force at Pointe-du-Hoc played a significant role in weakening the German counterattacks against the exposed 116th RCT positions in Vierville.

The first platoons to arrive from 12./GR.726 and 3./GR 914 launched an attack around 1600hrs from the western side of Pointe-du-Hoc, anchored on the western Flak bunker, which hit the overextended Co F line. The German attack was broken up by accurate 60mm mortar fire. Around the same time, a German platoon almost stumbled into the Co D defenses on the Grandcamp road, but the Rangers held their fire and the Germans passed by without recognizing the Ranger positions.

As dusk approached, Rudder still had no news of the situation on Omaha Beach. Lt Eikner redoubled efforts to establish communications with the 116th RCT and V Corps, as well as to ensure continuous communication with the naval bombardment group at sea. Around 1500hrs, a message was received from the 116th RCT, but merely noting that they had been unable to understand the Ranger radio message. The situation on the defensive perimeter was not good, as the men were running out of ammunition due to the loss of the two supply craft and the relatively light loads carried individually by the Rangers. There was no food available beyond the single "D-bar" chocolate ration carried by each soldier. Many Rangers began collecting German weapons to serve as a back-up when their own weapons were out of ammunition. Co E had two German MG34 and one MG42 machine-guns in operation by early evening.

JUNE 7 1944

0100hrs: Second German attack against Ranger advance detachment on the Grandcamp road

On D-Day, the destroyer USS *Thompson*, commanded by LtCmdr Albert Gebelin from Destroyer Division 36, bombarded the radar stations at *Stützpunkt Le Guay*. She relieved the *Satterlee* off Pointe-du-Hoc at 1840hrs, and defended the Rangers on the night of June 6–7 during the early-morning German attacks on Pointe-du-Hoc. Having fired all of her ammunition, *Thompson* had to retire around 0600hrs to replenish ammunition stocks, as seen here alongside the battleship USS *Arkansas*. (NARA)

By nightfall, the advance position to the south of the Grandcamp road numbered about 85 men, after the miraculous reinforcement by Parker's platoon from the 5th Rangers. The forward defensive position was reorganized shortly before dark into an L-shaped line 700 yards long located behind hedgerows oriented towards the southwest; Sgt Petty and a half-dozen other men were left in a forward outpost about 200 yards in front of the main defensive line. The night was clear with a nearly full moon; observation, however, to the south was poor, as the area at the junction of the "L" consisted of a pair of orchards bordered with hedgerows.

The German counterattack was repeatedly delayed during evening hours by naval bombardment from the destroyers off-shore. At 1950hrs, the Rangers requested the USS *Thompson* to deal with the concentration of troops from 3./GR.914 around the Château de M. la Baron near where the guns had been found. The first salvo was a direct hit on the buildings, and so the company waited until dark to stage their attack. Another strike was called in on seven targets at 2230hrs, shortly before nightfall.

The 3./GR.914 began its attack against the Ranger advance detachment near the Grandcamp road shortly after nightfall around 2330hrs. The Germans advanced almost to the edge of the Ranger defensive line before the officers began blowing whistles and ordering the assault. A confused, short-range skirmish ensued, which was interrupted after a few minutes when a powder explosion occurred in the hidden gun battery positions, now behind German lines. The Germans withdrew, having located the main Ranger defensive line. Casualties among the Co E Rangers holding the junction of the "L" weakened this critical position, and the attack made clear how precarious the defenses were at night when observation was so difficult and communication along the scattered Ranger line nearly impossible.

The second attack at 0100hrs began much like the first, with large amounts of German tracer fire and inaccurate mortar fire behind the Ranger line, followed by whistles and shouting. Once again, the German infantrymen were able to get to within 50 yards of the Rangers' line before being spotted. The attack again hit Co E, slightly to the east of the first attack. The attack succeeded in overrunning the angle at the

base of the "L," but the officers at the command post on the east side of the line had no communication with Co D, and no real information about the status of Co E. Since there was no reserve, there was no effort made to re-establish the position.

At 0300hrs, the third attack began, following the same pattern of machine-gun and mortar fire followed by whistles and shouted orders. The German attack broke through the Co E positions to the east of the angle, and after a few minutes German machine-gun teams began to pour enfilade fire along the inside of the hedgerow line. Scattered groups of Rangers, cut off and in some cases out of ammunition, began surrendering. In total, the Germans captured about 20 Rangers. The fighting proved to be just as confusing to the Germans. One soldier, Corp Karl Wegner, later recalled that "during the night, the Rangers would attack and infiltrate our lines, even though we vastly outnumbered them … when we attacked we learned that they were good fighters all around." The "infiltration" mentioned was the result of the scattered actions of Rangers like the indefatigable Sgt Petty, who made his way back to Pointe-du-Hoc on his own, ambushing unsuspecting German patrols from the rear.

The Rangers from Co F and the 5th Rangers around the command post began withdrawing after they were told that Cos E and D had been overrun. When they reached the Grandcamp road, Lt Robert Arman made a quick survey of the survivors and found that most of Co F was present, but few men from either Co D or Co E. Arman's group headed back into the Pointe-du-Hoc battery position along the access road, while the 5th Ranger platoon infiltrated back in small groups. About 50 of the 85 Rangers made it back to Pointe-du-Hoc and a hasty defense was set up in a line from gun pit 5 to gun pit 3. About a dozen Rangers from Co D were still in their fox-holes along the hedgerows, but in light of the German advance decided to remain hidden until daylight. A number of other Rangers remained hidden in scattered positions for the next few days. By daylight on D+1, Rudder's force had fallen from the original 200 Rangers to about 90 men able to bear arms. There are no known German records of strength or casualties during the fighting.

The preliminary casualty count of the 2nd Rangers on D-Day and the early morning hours of D+1 was 78 killed, 131 wounded, and 24 prisoners-of-war or missing for a total of 233 men of the original 545 Rangers; in other words, 43 percent casualties. The D-Day casualties suffered by the three companies that had landed on Omaha Beach were heavier than those suffered by the three companies at Pointe-du-Hoc: 84 wounded and 52 killed on Dog Green compared to 47 wounded, 26 killed, and 23 prisoners-of-war at Pointe-du-Hoc.

The German counterattack against Pointe-du-Hoc ground to a halt around daylight as it was subjected to naval gunfire. Skirmishing continued, however, and both sides set up defensive positions along the perimeter and harassed each other with machine-gun fire and mortars. The Ranger positions were reinforced by removing Lewis guns from the beached Ladder-DUKWs and the damaged LCAs. In addition, all German weapons were located and issued where needed. The defensive line included not only the Rangers, but British LCA crews and a few 101st Airborne paratroopers who had dropped near Pointe-du-Hoc. Communications between the command post and the naval bombardment group improved, and the Rangers were able to rely on continual naval gunfire support throughout D+1.

The predicament of the Rangers on Pointe-du-Hoc was exacerbated by the lack of communication with Army HQ on Omaha Beach. When Rudder relieved Maj Lytle, he did not appoint another Ranger officer to take his place on the command ship USS *Ancon*. This omission broke a key link in the chain-of-command. The US Navy had a good appreciation of the status of the Rangers on Pointe-du-Hoc, while the Army did not; a Ranger liaison officer could have bridged this gap. The senior

Army commanders from First Army, V Corps, 1st and 29th Infantry Divisions, were all preoccupied with the desperate situation on Omaha Beach through much of D-Day, and not the fate of a few Ranger companies at Pointe-du-Hoc. The situation was further confused by the belated and prolonged transit of the corps and division HQs from the transport off-shore to Omaha Beach during the afternoon and evening of D-Day. As a result, on the morning of D+1, the senior Army commanders on Omaha Beach had no idea of the fate of Rudder's Rangers at Pointe-du-Hoc.

The last German position within the Pointe-du-Hoc perimeter was the observation bunker. Rudder instructed Lt Vermeer, the battalion demolition officer, to deal with the problem once and for all. Vermeer took a 20lb sack of C-2 explosive, and wedged it against the rear door of the bunker. The explosion ripped off the door, and the eight surviving Germans emerged. Vermeer led a patrol later in the afternoon to eliminate an ammo dump near the access road, which had fallen into German hands after the advance position had been lost the night before. The dump was being used by the western Flak bunker as a source of supply for 37mm ammo. Several Bangalore torpedoes were placed into the ammunition dump, setting off a major detonation.

During D+1, the first serious attempt began to re-supply the Rangers. One of Admiral Hall's staff with the 11th Amphibious Force, Maj Jack Street, had served as a company commander with the 1st Rangers in the Mediterranean operations and received permission to gather reinforcements. A number of Rangers had congregated on Omaha Beach, including the crews of Lt Frank Kennard's halftrack cannon platoon, and the 1st Platoon of Co F, 5th Rangers, who had arrived late due to a leaky craft. They were taken back out to sea, where they joined up with landing craft that were loaded with food and supplies. After an attempt in the morning to land an LCT on the beach failed due to the tides, four LCVPs reached Pointe-du-Hoc around 1500hrs. About 60 Rangers landed along with food, ammo, and supplies, and the landing craft evacuated 52 of the most seriously wounded Rangers as well as a number of German prisoners.

Rudder's Rangers prepare to depart Pointe-du-Hoc on D+2 after the arrival of the relief column. Rudder is in the center facing the camera. The sergeant with the Thompson submachine-gun is Jack Kuhn, and a medic from the 29th Division can be seen to the right.

The Crazy March to Pointe-du-Hoc

The horrendous casualties suffered by the 116th RCT in overcoming *Stützpunkt Vierville* on D-Day morning, and the repeated GR.916 counterattacks against the village of Vierville, delayed the start of a relief effort towards Pointe-du-Hoc until the morning of D+1. Late on D-Day, GR.916 had been reinforced with the divisional engineer battalion as well as the construction troops of *Landesbaupionere Bataillon 17*, and continued counterattacks after midnight, pushing the 121st Engineer Battalion out of Château de Vaumicel in the pre-dawn hours. Briefings prior to D-Day had stressed the probability of intense German counterattacks on D+1, so Col Canham reduced the size of the relief force intended for Pointe-du-Hoc, leaving four of the six 5th Ranger companies and two tank companies from the 743rd Tank Battalion back in the Vierville area to protect the town and the beach exit. Contributing to the lack of urgency in dispatching the relief force was the deficit of information about the fate of Rudder's Rangers at Pointe-du-Hoc, and the widespread suspicion that Rudder's men had been overrun after dark.

The relief force was directed by LtCol John Metcalfe, commander of the 1/116th Infantry. Around 0745hrs, the columns headed out from the Vierville area towards Pointe-du Hoc along the Vierville–Grandcamp road. The composite company of the surviving 2nd Rangers under Capt Edgar Arnold insisted on taking point, and were followed by ten M4 medium tanks of B/743rd Tank Battalion. The rest of the relief force consisted of about 250 soldiers of 1/116th Infantry, as well as Cos C and D of the 5th Rangers. The relief column made steady progress on the morning of D+1, advancing about 2 miles west of Vierville. The Rangers infiltrated past the few German positions along the road, and when resistance was encountered, the tanks came up and blasted through. The Germans were surprised by the advance, calling it the "crazy march," as the advancing relief column simply ignored the substantial German defensive positions along the sea.

The relief column reached St-Pierre-du-Mont, about a thousand yards from Pointe-du-Hoc, around 1100hrs. About 200 yards west of the village and past the Pointe-du-Hoc access road, the Rangers halted due to some large craters in the roads caused by the pre-landing bombardment, which they knew would stop the tanks. Capt Arnold sent runners back to the rear to get a tank-dozer to fill the craters. By this stage, the column was under intermittent but serious artillery fire, mainly from the Maisy batteries, which, unlike the artillery of the 352.Infanterie-Division, still had ample ammunition.

While waiting for the 1/116th Infantry and 5th Rangers to arrive, the officers began discussing the next course of action. From their vantage point near the access road into Pointe-du-Hoc, it appeared that Rudder's force had either been overwhelmed or had simply left. The relief force radioed for a naval fire support mission against Pointe-du-Hoc, but this was refused by the Navy, who for the first time confirmed that Rudder's Rangers were indeed still holding Pointe-du-Hoc. Attempts to push the force further down the road towards Grandcamp were frustrated by continued German artillery and mortar fire. From reports provided by French civilians, the NSFCP-3 accompanying the column called in naval fire on the two Maisy batteries and an 88mm Flak battery near Criqueville-en-Bessin. Using its spotter plane, USS *Texas* brought the batteries under fire around 1300–1400hrs and the artillery fire ceased. The effects of the various naval bombardments against the Maisy batteries is not certain. From prisoner-of-war accounts, both batteries had each lost two of their four guns by D+2.

JUNE 7 1944

0300hrs: Third German attack against Ranger advance detachment on the Grandcamp road

JUNE 7 1944

0745hrs: Relief column sets out for Pointe-du-Hoc along the Grandcamp road

During the course of the afternoon, an officer from the 29th Division came into the command post in St- Pierre-du-Mont and informed the ranking Ranger officers, Capts John Raaen (HQ) and Wilmer Wise (Co C), that Vierville had been retaken by the Germans, the beachhead in the Vierville sector liquidated, and that German Panzers were coming up the road behind the 5th Rangers. Since they had been warned that morning to expect German counterattacks with Panzer support, the news was treated seriously by the Rangers.

The Rangers were reluctant to return in spite of the reports of German counterattacks, and a force of Rangers and a contingent from 1/116th Infantry remained in St-Pierre-du-Mont, with defensive positions oriented southwest towards Vierville due to concern about the rumored threat. When Capt John Raaen walked to the perimeter to check on the disposition of the force facing Vierville, another 29th Division officer came up the road, nonchalantly pedaling a bicycle. He told Raaen that in fact there had been no German counterattack that day, and that the 175th Infantry of the 29th Division had landed and was moving up the Vierville ravine and might be coming up the road shortly. Although the rumor about the German counterattack was false, Col Canham remained worried about the situation around Vierville, so he ordered the tanks to return to refuel and replenish their ammunition.

Later in the day, the two surviving M3 75mm GMC halftracks of the 2nd Rangers' cannon platoon drove up to St-Pierre-du-Mont with supplies and ammunition. At 1700hrs, radio communication was finally made between Rudder's headquarters and C/5th Rangers, and Rudder radioed "Try to fight through to us." As the 5th Rangers were under the command of the 116th Infantry, they had to wait until given the go-ahead by Col Canham. Once Raaen was content with his defensive position in St-Pierre, he asked two men from C/5th Rangers, Sgt Willie Moody and Cpl Howard McKissick, to try to make contact with Rudder's Rangers by infiltrating through German lines after dark. They did so, and managed to connect a field telephone line between the 2nd Ranger position and the Rangers in St-Pierre-du-Mont.

After a day of considerable confusion, an unidentified officer of the 5th Rangers reported to V Corps G-2 (intelligence) around 1945 that the Germans had retaken Pointe-du-Hoc. Considering the numerous rumors that had been flying around that day, this was ignored, but the 116th Infantry decided to wait until daylight on D+2 for a final push to Pointe-du-Hoc. This time, the mission was not simply to relieve Pointe-du-Hoc, but to push on to Grandcamp and Isigny to link up Omaha and Utah Beaches. The forces assigned to the relief column on D+2 included Ranger Force C, all three battalions of the 116th Infantry, and 16 M4 medium tanks of Cos A and C, 743rd Tank Battalion.

The relief operation began with a preliminary bombardment of the German positions by the destroyer USS *Ellison* with 140 rounds from its 5in guns. Cos B and E, 5th Rangers, were assigned to move west and take the high ground on the western side of Grandcamp, while the rest of Force C and 1/116th Infantry moved directly on Pointe-du Hoc from the St-Pierre-du-Mont area. The main force led by A/743rd Tank Battalion and 3/116th Infantry headed down the Grandcamp road, then swung right toward the Pointe-du-Hoc access road followed by A/743rd Tank Battalion and 2/116th

An improvised grave of one of the Rangers on Pointe-du-Hoc. (NARA)

Infantry. The advance began at 1015hrs and was met with significant mortar fire. Rudder dispatched a patrol from Co F to attempt to link up with the approaching force on the access road, but they failed to meet.

The M4 tanks turned off the Grandcamp road and headed for Pointe-du-Hoc, ignoring the "Vorsicht Minen" ("caution mines") signs still left standing on the outer perimeter of the strongpoint; one tank was lost to a mine. As the main force reached the edge of the Rangers defensive positions at Pointe-du-Hoc around 1100hrs, the 3/116th Infantry began firing on the Ranger positions due to the distinctive sound of German machine-guns, not knowing that the Rangers were using captured German weapons. A wild melee broke out with tank fire and mortars, and the Rangers lost four killed and three wounded. A recognition flare was fired by the 2nd Rangers, and several men at the command post held an American flag aloft. In the meantime, Adm Carleton Bryant aboard USS *Texas* heard the firing and radioed to Rudder: "Are you being fired on?" Rudder replied "Yes." "Do you want me to fire on them?" Rudder answered "No." Bryant finally asked "Are you being hit by friendly fire?" Rudder replied "Yes." One of the tankers later described the operation as a "stumble-footed attack that hadn't been coordinated by the people in charge." After a half-hour of confusion, the firing finally quieted down. Col Canham radioed divisional HQ at 1135hrs that Pointe-du-Hoc had been secured. It is unclear how many German troops were still in the area when the relief column arrived; GR.914 had been withdrawing its forces behind the Vire River and there was little opposition.

During the clean-up operation on Pointe-du-Hoc, a number of scattered Ranger detachments that had remained hidden since the German attacks in the early morning hours of D+1 were finally able to come out of hiding and join up with the rest of the battalion. By the end of D+2, the 2nd Rangers casualties stood at 263, including 70 dead, out of the original 545 men.

Over a dozen Rangers received the Distinguished Service Cross for their actions on D-Day, including Rudder, and several are seen here after the ceremony. Amongst them are: LtCol Max Schneider, commander of the 5th Rangers; Maj Richard Sullivan (XO/5th); Capt Otto Masny (F/2nd); Capt Edgar Arnold (B/2nd); Capt Ralph Goranson (C/2nd); Lt Joseph Lacy (5th); Lt George Kerchner (D/2nd); Sgt John White (2nd); Sgt Julius Belcher (2nd), and Pvt William Dreher (2nd). (NARA)

ANALYSIS

The assault on Pointe-du-Hoc has become a military legend and a cornerstone in Ranger history – "Rangers, lead the way" has since become the Ranger motto. When President Ronald Reagan visited Normandy on the 40th anniversary in June 1984, the highlight was his dedication of the Ranger monument above the observation bunker. Amidst the numerous acts of heroism by US troops on D-Day, the valiant actions by the 2nd Rangers stood above the rest. Pointe-du-Hoc had become enshrined in legend. Controversy began to surround the popular image of the event with the publication of Cornelius Ryan's best-seller *The Longest Day* in 1959 and Daryl Zanuck's Oscar-winning film version that appeared in 1962. In the book, the raid was characterized as "heroic and futile," highlighting the fact that the guns were not on Pointe-du-Hoc. The film was bitterly criticized by Ranger veterans for not pointing out that the guns were found and destroyed and that they still posed a threat to Utah Beach. Was the Pointe-du-Hoc battery such a threat that it warranted such a risky raid? This can be answered from two perspectives: the contemporary perspective of the Allied planners in June 1944, and an assessment based on the historical evidence that has accumulated since 1944.

The Allied planners thought that the batteries were still operational prior to D-Day based on the best evidence available – the final assessment on May 29 of the most recent aerial reconnaissance photos. There have been rumors over the years that Rudder and Lytle were told on the night before D-Day that the guns had been moved, which was the cause of Lytle's drunken outburst on the HMS *Ben My Chree*. There

Cornelius Ryan's bestseller *The Longest Day* and Daryl Zanuck's Oscar-winning film adaptation began the controversy over Pointe-du-Hoc, labeling the raid "heroic and futile." This is a production still from the film, which was staged at the original locations on Pointe-du-Hoc. (MHI)

have been unsubstantiated stories about late-arriving intelligence from the French resistance. Curiously enough, Rudder never publicly commented on this prior to his death in 1970 nor have other senior Ranger officers. Surviving evidence in the archives, including the V Corps G-2 assessment and the US Navy intelligence assessment for D-Day, indicate that Allied intelligence still believed that the guns were ready for action prior to D-Day. Furthermore, it is questionable whether Allied planners would scuttle the Ranger raid at the last minute based on unconfirmed intelligence from France, when confirmed evidence in the form of aerial photographs suggested otherwise. It is quite possible that Rudder and the other senior Ranger officers were warned that the guns might have been moved. Gen Omar Bradley later denied that the senior command of US First Army had any knowledge of the guns being removed. The evidence suggests that there may have been uncertainty about the guns, but not enough to derail the Ranger mission. Furthermore, had the mission gone as planned and the 5th Rangers landed in support of Force A, this more substantial force would have aided in V Corps' drive towards Grandcamp and Maisy and accelerated the link-up with Utah Beach.

In retrospect a half-century later, a case can be made that the Allied planners underestimated the potential of Operation *Flashlamp* and overestimated the capabilities of the Pointe-du-Hoc battery. As has been detailed in this book, the battery was crippled by the April 25 air raid and rendered inoperative by the RAF *Flashlamp* raid in the hours prior to the Ranger landings at Pointe-du-Hoc. Allied commanders did not know this at the time, and the *Flashlamp* raid might have proven to be as ineffective as the USAAF pre-dawn bombardment of Omaha Beach.

Allied intelligence overestimated the capabilities of the Pointe-du-Hoc battery due to a profound misunderstanding of its technical features and shortcomings. The failure of the Organization Todt to complete the gun casemates left the battery in exposed gun pits that made them extremely vulnerable to air attack and naval bombardment. Furthermore, the battery did not possess the type of plotting equipment necessary to engage moving naval targets, and the battery could not fire on targets beyond visual range, such as the vital Transport Area, except in the crudest fashion.

What sort of threat would Pointe-du-Hoc have posed if it had not been taken by the Rangers? Intriguing evidence is provided by the widely ignored experience of her sister battery, 4./HKAA.1260, to the east of Omaha Beach at Longues-sur-Mer. This was a Kriegsmarine rather than a Heer coastal battery and so had much better plotting and observation equipment, which did give it the capability to engage moving naval targets. It was by far the most sophisticated coastal battery on the Calvados coast, and its four 150mm guns were in full casemates on D-Day. Interestingly enough, it was also in range of Omaha Beach, which was 6–10 miles away; its maximum effective range was 12 miles. Yet Allied planners recognized the threat it posed too late because

JUNE 7 1944

1500hrs: Ranger reinforcements land at Pointe-du-Hoc

JUNE 8 1944

1135hrs: Pointe-du-Hoc secured

President Ronald Reagan's commemoration of the Ranger memorial on top of the observation bunker at Pointe-du-Hoc was the centerpiece of the American D-Day anniversary in Normandy in June 1984. Several of the surviving Rangers were in attendance. (US Department of Defense)

the battery was not completed until May 1944; instead of a special forces raid it was attacked solely by air attack and naval bombardment, the alternative that could have been applied to Pointe-du-Hoc.

The experience of Longues-sur-Mer provides a strong hint of what might have happened at Pointe-du-Hoc without the Ranger raid. Like Ponte-du-Hoc, Longues-sur-Mer was subjected to intense pre-invasion bombing, culminating in a *Flashlamp* raid in the pre-dawn hours. The bombing raids damaged one of its four casemates, and tore up the electrical cabling between the guns and the fire direction center, incapacitating its high-tech fire control system. The battery was then subjected to bombardment by the cruiser HMS *Ajax*, which had less effect. Around dawn, the battery opened fire on the command ship HMS *Bulolo* so HMS *Ajax* returned along with the HMS *Argonaut* and began pounding the battery again, firing some 179 rounds. The battery ceased fire around 0845hrs after two of its guns were knocked out by direct hits through the open embrasures, and the other two guns were temporarily out of action due to dirt and debris thrown up against the embrasures by the explosions and the pre-dawn bombardment. The gun crews spent much of the morning trying to get some guns operational again, and in the afternoon the remaining two guns opened fire towards the landing areas off Omaha Beach. The French cruiser *Georges Leygues*, which was defending the American sector, turned its fire on the battery, silencing it again. The battery fired some 115 rounds during the course of the day without hitting anything and was finally overrun by British infantry from Gold Beach on D+1. It is unlikely that Pointe-du-Hoc would have done any better than Longues-sur-Mer, especially since its exposed guns would have been far more vulnerable to naval counter-battery fire than the casemated guns of Longues-sur-Mer. The USS *Texas* had its spotter planes aloft on D-Day and could have located the Pointe-du-Hoc battery whether in the orchard or in the gun pits.

This famous photo was taken by a Navy photographer in the area of Rudder's command post on D+2 after Pointe-du-Hoc was relieved. Lt Eikner can be seen in the center drinking from a canteen, and Commando observer LtCol Thomas Trevor can be seen in the lower right with his bandaged head from a wound suffered during the initial landings. (NARA)

The idea that the Pointe-du-Hoc battery posed an overwhelming threat to the troops on either Omaha or Utah Beach is largely a misunderstanding that has been fostered in several histories of the Ranger operation. The main concern of Allied planners was the threat it posed to the amphibious transport ships while they were off-loading troops in the Transport Area in the pre-dawn hours. It is often overlooked that Omaha Beach was subjected to the fire of two howitzer batteries of the 352.Infanterie-Division, which had pre-registered the beach exits in the months before the landing, and which had forward observers on the beach to correct their fire. In addition, Werfer-Regiment 84 was located inland of the St Laurent ravine and was able to fire its massive artillery rockets all day long. These batteries posed a much greater hazard to the troops on Omaha Beach than the guns on Pointe-du-Hoc. While Allied intelligence recognized the Pointe-du-Hoc and Longues-sur-Mer batteries as potential hazards to the troops on Omaha Beach, this was not the primary reason for the Ranger mission.

In hindsight, with the evidence available today, the raid on Pointe-du-Hoc was probably not necessary. But for the Allied commanders in June 1944, with the incomplete and inaccurate intelligence assessments they had at hand, the raid was a prudent use of special operations forces to deal with what was perceived as a significant threat. The performance of Ranger Force A was exemplary, and reinforcement by Force C at Pointe-du-Hoc proved unnecessary to carry out the primary mission. Indeed, it can be argued that the dispatch of Force C to its secondary mission on Omaha Beach had much more beneficial results for the outcome of the US operations on Omaha Beach than had it landed to reinforce Force A. The momentum of the 5th Ranger advance over the bluff east of Vierville was a major factor in redeeming the 116th Infantry assault after the bloodbath in the kill-zone of Strongpoint Vierville.

For the troops of the 2nd Rangers, Pointe-du-Hoc was their solitary moment in the limelight. The battalion received the Presidential Unit Citation for their actions on D-Day; at least 14 soldiers of the 2nd Rangers received the Distinguished Service Cross for their individual actions in Normandy. While Pointe-du-Hoc later became the stuff of legend, there was little jubilation amongst the Rangers in the aftermath of the attack. Few of these young citizen-soldiers had seen combat before D-Day, and in spite of their training they were stunned by the shock of war and its cruel casualties. There were no parades or celebrations, only more training and the incorporation of new men to take the places of many fallen. For all their preparation and sacrifices, the Rangers were largely without a mission after D-Day. As LtGen McNair had argued in 1942, small elite light infantry were not a comfortable fit with US Army doctrine of the time. Senior commanders like Gen Bradley were unwilling to risk such highly trained troops on regular infantry duty, yet the Rangers lacked the mobility of mechanized cavalry or airborne forces for other special missions. The 2nd Rangers were eventually committed to action in Brittany in the late summer of 1944 and in the Hürtgen forest fighting in December 1944, where they again suffered significant casualties but for far less dramatic or important missions. It was only in the decades after the war that the US Army began to re-think its requirements for elite light infantry, especially in low-intensity conflicts. The indelible legend of Rudder's Rangers at Pointe-du-Hoc helped inspire this later revival of the Rangers.

FURTHER READING

The raid on Pointe-du-Hoc has been widely covered in books about the Rangers and D-Day. The first and most significant study was contained in the chapter in the 1946 US War Department study *Small Unit Actions*, the outcome of the Army's wartime "Combat Interviews" program. It is not widely known that the unpublished version of the study contains some significant differences from the published version and that it included an unpublished second part covering Force B and Force C as well as the D+1 and D+2 relief effort. The original hand-written draft of this study is located at the US National Archives and Records Administration (NARA) in College Park, Maryland. Few of the Rangers penned their own accounts of the battle, and the absence of a memoir by Col Rudder is all the more surprising in view of his academic career. Nevertheless, there is an extensive first-person record created over the years from numerous interviews with Ranger veterans, contained in the books mentioned below.

Other unit records consulted for this book at NARA included the after-action-reports and journals of the 2nd Rangers, 5th Rangers, 743rd Tank Battalion, 116th Infantry Regiment, the V Corps G-2, and the SHAEF G-2 "Martian" Reports. The *Kriegstagebücher* (war-diaries) of the LXXXIV Corps and 352.Infanterie-Division are missing for the months prior to and including D-Day, but the 1943 records at NARA were consulted as well as the 1944 records of the German Seventh Army in Normandy.

Another significant archival source on Pointe-du-Hoc is the US Army's Military History Institute (MHI) at Carlisle Barracks, Pennsylvania. MHI has two notable resources: the Robert Rowe collection contains a substantial amount of documents on the naval aspects of Pointe-du-Hoc, and a large number of personal recollections by Ranger veterans; MHI also has the collection of the informal 2nd Ranger historian, Louis Lisko, who was a radioman in Rudder's HQ at Pointe-du-Hoc.

Aside from some maddeningly incomplete remarks in Stjernfelt's early study, accounts of Pointe-du-Hoc from the German perspective were largely lacking until the publication of Von Kuesgen's book in 2006, which includes the recollections of several surviving veterans, including one of the machine-gunners from Werfer-Regiment 84 and a radio-man from the command bunker. In spite of the loss of so many of the primary sources on German actions on D-Day, Hans Sakker has compiled the surviving German diaries and other documents into his essential compendium *Normandie 6.Juni 1944*.

The 4./HKAR.1260 battery at Longues-sur-Mer on the opposite side of Omaha Beach provides a counter-factual argument about the need for the Ranger raid on Pointe-du-Hoc. The battery was naval pattern with full casemates and armed with 150mm destroyer guns behind armored shields. (Author)

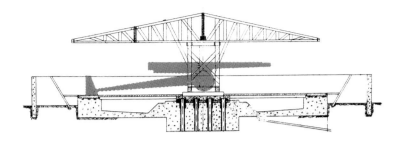

The guns in the Pointe-du-Hoc battery were covered with camouflage umbrellas in the summer of 1943. These were wooden structures erected over the kettle position to support camouflage netting. The presence of this camouflage umbrella hiding the guns made it almost impossible for Allied intelligence's aerial reconnaissance to determine whether they were actually present in the gun pits. This is an original drawing from one of the "Martian" reports prepared by Allied intelligence in London on German Normandy defenses. (NARA)

Simon Trew of the Royal Military Academy Sandhurst was kind enough to provide me with his notes from his extensive archival research at the UK National Archives in Kew, with especially helpful material on air operations and Operation *Flashlamp*.

n.a., *Small Unit Actions* (Historical Division, US War Department, 1946)

n.a., *Battle Summary No. 39: Operation "Neptune" Landings in Normandy, June 1944* (UK Naval Historical Branch, 1944; republished in *Invasion Europe*, HMSO, 1994)

Black, Robert, *The Battalion: The Dramatic Story of the 2nd Ranger Battalion in World War II* (Stackpole, 2006)

Ewing, Joseph, *29 Let's Go!: A History of the 29th Infantry Division in World War II* (Infantry Journal, 1948)

Gawne, Jonathan, *Spearheading D-Day: American Special Units in Normandy* (Histoire & Collections, 1998)

Glassman, Henry, *Lead the Way, Rangers: A History of the 5th Ranger Battalion* (private, 1946)

Hogan, David, *US Army Special Operations in World War II* (US Army Center for Military History, 1992)

Howard, Peter, *Pointe du Hoc* (Ian Allen, 2006)

Keusgen, Helmut Konrad von, *Pointe du Hoc* (Heimdal, 2006)

Kirkland, William, *Destroyers at Normandy: Naval Gunfire Support at Omaha Beach* (Naval Historical Foundation, 1994)

Lane, Ronald, *Rudder's Rangers: The True Story of the 2nd US Ranger Battalion's D-Day Combat Action* (Ranger Associates, 1979)

Lock, J. D., *Rangers in Combat* (Wheatmark, 2007)

McDonald, JoAnna, *The Liberation of Pointe du Hoc: The 2nd Rangers at Normandy: June 6–8, 1944* (Rank and File, 2000)

Milano, Vince, *Normandiefront: D-Day to St Lo through the German Eyes* (Spiess, 1994)

Morison, Samuel, *History of US Naval Operations in World War II: Vol. XI – The Invasion of France and Germany 1944–45* (Little & Brown, 1957)

Prince, M., *Co A, 2nd Rangers Battalion: Overseas and Then Over the Top We Went* (private, 1947)

Sakkers, Hans, *Normandie 6.Juni 1944 im Spiegel der deutschen Kriegstagebücher* (Biblio, 1998)

Shores, Christopher and C. Thomas, *2nd Tactical Air Force: Volume 1 – Spartan to Normandy June 1943 to June 1944* (Classic, 2004)

Stjernfelt, Bertil, *Alerte sur le mur de l'Atlantique* (Presses de la Cite, 1961)

Taylor, Thomas, *Rangers – Lead the Way* (Turner, 1996)

Zaloga, Steven, *D-Day Fortifications in Normandy* (Osprey, 2005).

INDEX

References to illustrations are shown in **bold**.